HUMAN RELATIONS
IN MANAGEMENT

HUMAN RELATIONS IN MANAGEMENT

BY

E. W. HUGHES, M.A., B.Sc.

MEMBER OF THE DIRECTING STAFF
ASHORNE HILL COLLEGE, LEAMINGTON

PERGAMON PRESS

OXFORD · NEW YORK · TORONTO
SYDNEY · BRAUNSCHWEIG

PERGAMON PRESS LTD.,
Headington Hill Hall, Oxford

PERGAMON PRESS INC.,
Maxwell House, Fairview Park, Elmsford, New York 10523

PERGAMON OF CANADA LTD.,
207 Queen's Quay West, Toronto 1

PERGAMON PRESS (AUST.) PTY. LTD.,
19a Boundary Street, Rushcutters Bay, N.S.W. 2011, Australia

VIEWEG & SOHN GMBH,
Burgplatz 1, Braunschweig

First edition 1970

Library of Congress Catalog Card No. 79–118838

Printed in Great Britain by A. Wheaton & Co., Exeter

08 015862 5 (flexicover)
08 015863 3 (hard cover)

TO MARION, JOHN AND HELEN
—for their patience and continued inspiration

This book is written for practising industrial and educational personnel. It attempts to show that it is possible to structure real life experiences and occasional research findings and arrive at a number of tentative working laws about people which can be used to predict behaviour in future situations. It relies very much on the analysis of actual experiences and not to a great extent on the collation of texts.

The form is apt to become a little personalized in attempting this structuring of experiences, but it is hoped that this approach will encourage the reader to search his own experience for similar evidence of principles of human behaviour.

The techniques employed have been developed over the last 20 years in teaching industrial and educational psychology on short courses.

A number of course members and colleagues have tried to persuade me to reproduce my lectures in book form and at last I have attempted it. I hope that this text captures some of the enthusiasm and obvious interest which this subject generates in study groups.

Contents

Acknowledgements

I SHOULD like to thank all those people in Industry, Education and the Profession who, in discussion or writing, have influenced my thinking about human relations over the past 30 years.

I am grateful to Jane Pilgrim and the Brockhampton Press for the theme of the book *Postman Joe* in the Blackberry Farm Series and also to the originator of the Job Breakdown Sheet of the T.W.I.—J.I. Programme, which I have quoted.

I very much appreciate the help and advice of Mr. J. H. McMillan, Mrs. P. Ducker and Mrs. S. Wright, of Pergamon Press, on the form and content of this book, and I wish to thank Miss C. Cooper and Miss L. V. Green for help in the preparation of the manuscript and references.

Finally I want to thank my wife for her help with the correction of proofs and for her valuable comments and support throughout the preparation of the book.

Introduction

Psychology—Mystery, Magic, Psychiatry?

OVER the past 20 years I have found myself involved in a great deal of short-course work with management, supervisory and professional groups on human relations topics and industrial psychology. I have found it necessary, in the early stages, to do something to help resolve the confusion which exists in course members' minds about psychology and psychiatry, and to dispel the aura of mystery, magic, superstition, and fear which exists on the one hand, or contempt and ridicule which is apparent on the other. Such phrases as: ". . . I've tried psychology and now I am going to use the big stick"; ". . . I know you are psycho-analysing us"; ". . . what we want is a psychological approach"; ". . . whatever you do don't mention psychology"; ". . . all right in theory but no use in practice" all illustrate the exaggerated attitudes which the lecturer in the human relations field is likely to meet and which I always try to anticipate in early contacts with a group.*

In Industrial Training it is quite common to be faced with something like 300–400 years industrial experience round the table. What can we do in these circumstances? How can we possibly help these experienced people to become more effective in future in the light of the weight of industrial experience available in the group? Should we teach a subject called industrial

* "So we must not be surprised if inspectors of technical instruction or professors of mechanical engineering, in the 20th century, regard the study of psychology as strange. But eventually the time will come when it will no longer be strange for technologists to think about the human beings who work for them or even, indeed, to think a little about themselves; they could hardly make human relations in some enterprises any worse by doing so." (R. W. Revans, *Science and the Manager*, MacDonald, London, 1965, p. 142.)

psychology? Are we really concerned with a body of knowledge or are we concerned, rather, with attitude? These are vital questions to answer.

Behaviour the Key

In management, essentially, we are trying to understand and influence the mental processes of others and therefore as social scientists must ask ourselves: What access have we to the mental processes of others? How do we really know what is going on in another person's mind?

The answer, of course, is that in the absence of telepathy (i.e. extra-sensory communication), the only access we have to the mental processes of others is via a study of their behaviour. In fact the most remarkable thought process there has ever been has only communicated itself to the outside world by a muscular contraction—a half-smile, a gesture, an odd word, or a rapid jotting. A draughtsman once told me that he reckoned to have a 10-minute nap every afternoon, but if anyone came anywhere near his board, he wrote a number 6 on the paper. We have now no evidence of what he had been doing. Had he been thinking hard over the last 10 minutes and was the 6 the end product of his thinking? Was he really dozing, or was he miles away following a train of thought nothing to do with his work? This shows that in describing a work situation it is not sufficient for an outside observer to report precisely on what he sees; it is also necessary for the individual himself to do some introspection about his own behaviour.

This has important implications for the design of selection and training programmes, because it is the *intellectual* demands, as well as *physical* demands which a task makes on a person which are important. We cannot observe the intellectual demands of a task on another, and accordingly cannot escape from some subjective judgements.

Generally, then, the psychologist is a student of behaviour—of others and his own. His basic raw material is behaviour.

Every Man is a Psychologist

This makes everyone a psychologist in the sense that everyone is a student of behaviour. We know the significance of that slight frown. We know when people are laughing with us and not at us. We can detect the genuine applause—the warning note—the sincere letter. In fact we have been studying the behaviour of other people all our lives in an attempt to manipulate them to our advantage or to elicit support for a cause. And we have been so successful in doing this that we have managed to stay alive in a very complex society.

It is no figure of speech when I say "Every man is a psychologist" but the problem which this statement now raises is: What, then, is the contribution of the specialist (consultant) in this field?

Method in the Physical and Social Sciences

A parallel from the physical sciences can help us here. The working laws in physics, chemistry, metallurgy, and the like have been obtained by people fitting theories to explain the observations they had made about the properties of matter—a process of inductive reasoning, venturing hypotheses to fit observations. These theories are then strengthened by trying them out in new situations using the processes of deductive reasoning, aimed at verification, i.e. if this hypothesis is true then if I do this, such-and-such should happen—deduction and hoping for verification. This kind of process goes on until an event occurs which does not fit the existing hypothesis, and so the working law is modified to accommodate the new evidence. For example, in 1800 Dalton was able to say that atoms were indivisible and no one challenged him. But, of course, today, in the light of new evidence available, no one would support this assertion.

Thus in the physical sciences our working laws have been arrived at as a result of people systematizing and structuring what they had observed, using the processes of inductive reasoning, deductive reasoning, and verification. They are not certainties but probabilities—the best guess to date. In the social sciences, then, if we want any working laws about people we shall have to do the same, and so the contribution of the industrial psychologist (the consultant) is not to come along to tell people what to do, but to help experienced people to systematize and structure what they already know about the behaviour of people in industry. There is no mystery, no magic, but straightforward common sense in this approach. The methods of teaching must value the experience of the members of the group and provide working situations where the experiences can be pooled readily and effectively.

Two very important points arise from this approach:

(a) Management training must be a postgraduate activity in the sense that the course members must have had some experience of an appropriate nature to structure; and

(b) the activity is essentially a research activity and not the activity of teaching a body of knowledge.

The individuals will be structuring their own experiences—arriving at working conclusions about their own experiences—working in a transfer situation and not applying a law which they have been taught as an abstract.

End-on Courses

This means that "end-on" courses in colleges and universities need to adopt a different method from that used for experienced people. Case histories and role-playing situations have to be employed to provide vicarious experiences which can then be used to *illustrate principles* and *practise techniques*. There will be something unreal about this and an impression of "This is what happens to other people". The "postgraduate" activity, i.e. activity with experienced people and its syndicate methods of working (structuring own experiences) will, in contrast, be real and "happen to me".

Not a Subject

In brief, psychology to me has to be related to living in this world. Every approach is a psychological approach (but, of course, some approaches are better thought out than others).

I believe that if we teach a body of knowledge then there is a tendency for this to become an abstraction divorced from reality, leading furthermore to a tendency to expect people to conform to this norm. The deviate now becomes *wrong* instead of an accepted part of the set-up of which the generalization is the norm.

If, however, we adopt the other position of probabilities and of structuring experiences, then the deviate is recognized as one of the possible elements in the situation. Again, in approaching a new situation, the attitude is not one of applying a rigid law and of requiring behaviour of a given type but more the attitude "This has happened in the past (say very often), I wonder whether it will happen again in this new situation?"

I believe this emphasis on probability rather than certainty, is the more realistic approach even in the physical sciences, and it is for this reason I prefer to think of attempting a "science of human relations" rather than a subject called industrial psychology. The chapters in this book will maintain this inductive emphasis rather than the body of knowledge and deductive emphasis because:

(a) I believe this to be the only procedure tenable, and
(b) it ensures maximum transfer of experience and minimizes resistance to change.

In staff training we hope that people attending courses will try their ideas against those of other course members, the lecturers, and any other material in books, papers, or various aids, and will go away more convinced than ever about the position they hold on certain issues, or, because of something new they have experienced for the first time, will have changed their viewpoint slightly.

No one can predict the actual situations in which the manager/supervisor will find himself, and so the best we can do is to help him have confidence in his own ability to recognize a problem and make decisions which advance its solution.

It is this kind of hope that I hold out in justification of this text, and if it achieves this purpose I will be well satisfied.

Content

The topics I have found in practice to be urgent are:

The implications of habit formation.
The background to incentives.
The problems of persuasion—attitude change.
The problems of communication.
The problems of personality, selection, and learning.
The question of industrial conditions as they relate to morale.

I have considered (and indeed in the past have used), three different approaches, via:

(i) A study of the basic concept of personality and the implications of personality traits for industry and education.
(ii) A study of the factors affecting productivity.
(iii) A study of industrial efficiency and morale.

For the purpose of this book I propose to follow the third approach:

Industrial efficiency and morale.

CHAPTER 1

Industrial Efficiency and Morale

THE efficient use of human resources is my main interest in staff training, and consequently I am concerned about those factors called fatigue and boredom which affect efficiency adversely. These terms get confused in conversation and analysis for the reason that the only condition we can observe in the individual is a state of reduced capacity for work. It is necessary then to tease out these terms a little in view of their importance in effective work.

Reduced Capacity for Work

Fatigue and Boredom

Some years ago I was due to lecture to a mining society in the north-west and was told by my sponsor to get off the train at a station about 5 miles from St. Helens and he would be there to meet me to give me a meal and take me to the place where I was to lecture. As advised, I got off the train at what I thought to be the station concerned, only to realize, as the train was pulling away, that it was the wrong station. I found myself with a large canvas bag some 4 ft by 3 ft, containing a number of heavy cardboard charts, and another case loaded with hand-out material, and so decided to call a taxi. But there were no taxis. Not beaten, I went to the nearest garage and said "What about running me to St. Helens?" The owner was sympathetic, seeing my load, but said that all his men were on urgent jobs and he could not really help me—and so there was no alternative but to walk.

Now 5 miles does not daunt me, but with the load I had it was not going to be easy; notwithstanding, off I set. After the first half mile or so the weight of the charts on my right hand began to get uncomfortable and so I adopted the obvious tactic of changing this bag from my right hand to the left hand because the effect was local and could be eased by changing hands. But when I had done this many times in the course of 5 miles, what had started off as a local effect finished as a general effect and I arrived at my destination in a state of considerable distress.

I might be tempted to define this state as illustrating fatigue—a state of reduced capacity for work brought about by previous activity of the same or a similar kind—I had been using muscles.

On the other hand, if you take young children for walks they sometimes complain of feeling tired and want to be carried home. If you now turn the rest of the journey home into a game, not only will they travel the distance but they will run round and round in circles and travel about ten times as far. This illustrates the problem of boredom—reduced capacity for work as a result of an unfavourable change in attitude towards the work situation.

Now let us examine my distressed state on arrival at St. Helens. Was my state of reduced capacity for work due to the fact that I had been using muscles or because I was "fed-up" with carrying the case in any event?

We shall never know and, what is more, we never will know in comparable circumstances; i.e. fatigue and boredom are combined in unknown proportions in all cases of reduced capacity for work.

If we improve the lighting in a workroom, people can "see better" and they also "feel better". Is the improvement in performance due to the fact that they can see better or feel better?

We have here the problem of situations where two adverse factors, combined in unknown proportions, are working simultaneously to reduce efficiency; then, obviously, in the interest of maximum efficiency we need to work at both to minimize their effects.

In order to counter losses on the physiological side, i.e. fatigue, we have the method study of the work study engineer. He is concerned with the efficient use of muscular activity. But this is not enough; someone must do something about the psychological state of the organism and be concerned with promoting favourable human relationships in the organization: this is often the immediate supervisor. And yet it is surprising how quite responsible courses in work study have treated the human relations topics as the "frills" of an otherwise technically sound programme of events.

As far as I am concerned, then, the method study engineer and the foreman are key personnel in promoting industrial efficiency via their attacks on losses originating in the physiological and psychological states of the organism.

Hawthorne Experiment

The argument above is reinforced and further developed in the reports from America on the work of Elton Mayo in the Hawthorne Plant of the Western Electric Company (late 1920's).

The Western Electric engineers had been experimenting with conditions of work in an attempt to improve efficiency, and had conducted experiments on lighting using an experimental group and a so-called control group to assess the effect of the changes they introduced.

They had improved the lighting in the experimental group and, as they expected, output had gone up; but it had gone up in the control group also, where, they said, they had done nothing.

This they could not understand, and so they had reduced the lighting in the experimental group and, very surprisingly indeed, output had gone up once more.

This completely puzzled the engineers: they could understand why output had gone up when they improved conditions but could not understand why output had gone up when they apparently did nothing (as with the control group), or, worse, had gone up when the conditions deteriorated.

At this stage they approached Harvard University and contacted an Australian psychologist named Elton Mayo.

Speaking at Birmingham (England) in the late 1940's, Mayo said that the engineers told him that they did not want him to tell them how to improve production—they knew how to do that: they wanted him to explain what had happened in their investigation.

Mayo and his colleagues went over to the Hawthorne Plant and worked on the problem for some 5 years, conducting a series of experiments. For one of the studies Mayo used a small team of workers assembling telephone relays. It is important to note that the workers had a little say, but not a complete say, as to who should be in the working team, and they were kept informed and were consulted, as appropriate, by a regular observer. A useful summary of this series of experiments is given in *Social Psychology of Industry* by J. A. C. Brown (Pelican, 1954) pp. 70–72, and the general problem is discussed by Mayo himself in his books *Human Problems of an Industrial Civilization* (Harvard University Press, 1933) and *Social Problems of an Industrial Civilization* (Harvard University Press, 1945); but, briefly, Mayo brought about changes in the motivational state and the physiological state of the workers by introducing piecework systems of payment; inserting rest pauses at different times and of differing lengths; experimenting with the length of the working day; and the introduction of free meals. As we would predict from our earlier work on fatigue and boredom, he was able to show improvements in output except when frequent rest pauses broke the rhythm of work; but the extraordinary result at the end (when he returned to the primitive conditions at the beginning of the experiment— 48-hour week; no rest pauses; no piecework; no free meals) of an output level which rocketed to the highest ever, would have nonplussed many an observer, and certainly would not have been predicted by our analysis to date.

I can imagine Mayo's dilemma at this final stage and after 5 years' work (these people!) but his response was *it cannot be the conditions of work—some other factors must be operating.* His final explanation was that the workers had identified themselves closely with the purpose of the group—the morale in the group was high (it had been encouraged by having a say in the working group and being kept informed by the observer) and it was this identification with the purpose of the group—this interest in the experiments—which was at the bottom of the high level performance.* In brief, Mayo maintained *morale is more important than the physical conditions of work*. Thus work on the human relations side might be more important than an attack on work study aspects.

This aspect of Mayo's work really only reinforces what any supervisor knows from his own study of people—we can get good output in poor working conditions if the human relationships are good, but we can get poor output in very good working conditions if the human relations are bad.

Other work in the Hawthorne investigation also showed that this identification of people working in groups may not necessarily be with the purpose of management, but with other interests, leading to an informal organization different from the formal one. The morale in the informal organization can still be high; but this time to the detriment of management and the supervisor, resulting in restrictive or protective practices (depending on which side you are on). For the moment I am interested in the importance of morale in this identification aspect irrespective of with which side it is concerned. I would argue that in the end it is the problem of management to try to maintain a balance in a number of conflicting interests,† not necessarily two sides but many sides, and for the moment am inclined to accept the view that morale is more important than the physical conditions of work in determining productivity.

(This Hawthorne Effect has become very important in research

* "It is probable that the second factor—the awareness of the experiment and of the need for increased output for its success—was an important cause of increased production." (Michael Argyle, The relay assembly rest room in retrospect, *Occupational Psychology*, April 1953, p. 100.)

† See Alan Fox, Managerial ideology and labour relations, *British Journal of Industrial Relations*, 4, 366–78 (1966).

work with groups of people. The identification of individuals with the purpose of a project can be more important than any other single variable in determining performance level. This throws great doubt on the use of control groups in social experiments because it is impossible to isolate this social psychological factor arising from the face-to-face relationships existing in the group. For this reason some of us prefer repeated research with intact groups rather than sampling research in the social sciences.)

Ergonomics (Classical)

So far our inquiry into factors affecting industrial efficiency has shown the importance of method study and human relations in determining maximum performance, but the situation is further complicated by research work during the Second World War and, since, on studies of conditions of work. Some of these were conducted in the University of Cambridge in the Applied Psychology Research Unit at Downing Place.

F. C. Bartlett* was running a research team looking into conditions of work and Dr. Mackworth was specializing on temperatures and humidity in submarines, engine rooms of ships, and the like. Around 1950 he produced findings which suggested that whilst individuals adjusted themselves to quite a fair range of temperatures around 65°F without significant deterioration in output, if the temperature exceeded 93°F with a humidity saturation of the order of 65 per cent, then output declined irrespective

---

* Emeritus Professor Sir Frederick Bartlett, "Human functions have been developed in a world of change. They will stand up to variability over a certain range with very little fluctuation. Quite large variations of environment within this range will affect human efficiency hardly at all. Quite small variations outside this range may make human activity markedly more or less effective. For many conditions of this order—heat and humidity, for example —the range has been firmly established; but for many more it has still to be found" (Men, machines and productivity, *Occupational Psychology*, **22** (4), October 1948).

of the incentives operating. This was true for quite a range of activities—light sedentary to heavy manual work.*

Bartlett suggested that this represented a human tolerance limit, arguing that the human being is a physical–chemical machine which will not work efficiently outside certain conditions: conditions in excess of these were true of some British industries, and we should try to work inside these tolerance limits. Research work in connection with abnormal working conditions such as are involved in projecting people into space at high velocities, has focused attention on the study of the physical and physiological limitations of the human beings in all conditions, normal and abnormal, and so a science called ergonomics‡ has now assumed a recognized place in the field. Some people say it is concerned with fitting a job to a person as opposed to selection, which is concerned with finding a person to suit a job. I prefer to define ergonomics‡ as the study of the physical and physiological limitations of the human being in the work situation.

Elton Mayo's statement now needs qualifying and the picture seems to be: *morale is more important than the physical conditions of work—within Bartlett's human tolerance limits.*

Three Fields of Study

To date, then, a real life incident has been used to illustrate the importance of method study and human relations in countering fatigue and boredom and thus promoting efficiency. The more formalized work of Elton Mayo has emphasized the morale aspect of human relations, and the later work of Bartlett's team has

* "Dr. Mackworth—he showed that for a large range of operations extending from heavy physical work with little skill, through highly skilled work with little physical effort at all, *significant deterioration sets in when the temperature is raised to about 93°F with a humidity saturation of about 65 per cent* in fully acclimatized workers. Those are conditions certainly not unknown in mining and other industries in this country." (F. C. Bartlett, Incentives, *British Journal of Psychology*, General Section, December 1950.)

† Term attributed to K. F. H. Murrell around 1949; see *Ergonomics*, Chapman & Hall, 1965, Preface, p. viii.

‡ Postgraduate courses and M.Sc. courses now exist.

pointed the field of ergonomics and the study of the interface between the human operator and the hardware systems.

There are thus three fields of study if we are considering the efficient use of human resources:

Method study, Ergonomics, Human relations.

The method study engineer is concerned with using a human machine in conjunction with other machines to get maximum effect. The ergonomics expert—the ergonomist—is concerned with what the human machine can stand and what are its strengths and limitations. But unlike all other machines the human machine might decide not to work: hence the study of what motivates him—the study of human relations.

This delimitation of the activities of the ergonomist will depend very much on word usage in particular establishments.* For example, some see the whole field of industrial psychology and the study of work as the field of ergonomics, and some industrial psychologists have labelled their departments accordingly; however, the above usage seems to me to be useful and meaningful.

The Cranfield College of Aeronautics approach to the ergonomics problem is interesting:

> If you cannot afford a human factors specialist then why not invest in a "cook book–recipe book, approach"—a reference work detailing research findings, e.g. on display panels, dials, and the like, indicating the degree of confidence with which the statements are made, i.e. the extent of experimental support.

It is well to bear in mind F. C. Bartlett's recommendation: *Design machines with an average man in mind, not a superman.*

At this stage I have made the case for method study, ergonomics. and a systematic study of human relationships. In this particular text we will be concerned with human relationships in the main. Many people have subscribed to this as being a problem area. They say "What we want is better human relationships"; but the problem is How do we get better human relationships? The work of the next four chapters suggests how this might be achieved by attempting to structure human relationships.

* See Singleton, Shuckel, Jackson, and Corlett, Why ergonomics?, *Occupational Psychology*, **41** (1), January 1967.

CHAPTER 2

The Implications of Habit Formation

I HAVE worked in several staff training establishments where it was customary for the members of the teaching staff to gather together to welcome new course members when they assembled for the first time. This meant allocating time to meeting new members and installing them in the establishment, sometimes at times which were domestically inconvenient, e.g. Sunday afternoons. In one case members of the staff had to be available for such reception work most of the day, because course members travelled from all over the British Isles and arrived at times which ranged widely. Now some of the members of the staff would complain, arguing that their job was lecturing or demonstrating and not that of a receptionist, and so it is reasonable to ask: Why bother about reception procedures?

Why Reception?

My immediate reply is "People form habits". They form habits very quickly in connection with the use of a particular establishment, and if you have any procedures which you want people to adopt, it is important to see that the approved procedures are known from the outset so that the approved habits can be perpetuated.

In one establishment the persons entering the dining room on the first night were told, "Sit where you like—there are no reserved or special seats." (There can be no special or reserved seats if you believe in the importance of pooling experiences in management training—no one is more important than anyone else. There

15

are odd exceptions to this rule, affecting domestic convenience, but in no way relating to status.) The next morning at breakfast a good many would return to the seat they first selected, but at lunch-time, owing to the arrival of more administrative staff, several members would find, to their concern, that someone had "taken their seat".

In discussing this problem of habits with course members it was possible to indicate the most likely best seats from the point of view of actual service (relying on the habits of the waitresses and the dining room layout). One group determined to prove me wrong and dropped a note to the waitresses asking them to serve in a different order. The result was fine at first, but ended in confusion because the waitresses got to a stage when they did not know whom they had served and where to go next—because they too had developed work habits.

We form habits in relation to the "pub" we use, the theatre we attend, possibly the newspaper we buy, and the cigarettes we smoke.

We can form bad habits in drving a car, in playing a musical instrument, in striking a ball, in using tools, and typing with two fingers.

A number of bank robberies have been based on the assumption of a particular routine and it is possible that certain habitual procedures are insisted upon in some establishments so that the individual's actions are likely to be appropriate when the stresses are such that he cannot think clearly, e.g. the Services.

Efficiency, Safety, Good Discipline

It is obvious then that if we know the most efficient movements required to do a job, we should receive new labour and teach them these procedures in order to establish efficient habits.

Once again, if we know the most safe methods of doing a job we should receive people and teach them the approved procedure, i.e. establish safe habits.

For example, they did not let me find out by trial and error how to behave in an explosives factory. They taught me safe methods of working from the outset, since some of my natural movements and normal handling procedures, and indeed clothing and personal possessions, were potentially dangerous. Considerable efforts were made to supplant these risky procedures and practices in the very early stages.

Again, in the mining industry, we found that pit-head bath superintendents on courses complained of bad discipline in the baths. Our first question was, Who received the new labour?, and this sometimes supplied the complete answer to the problem. *No one had made it clear from the outset what procedures were required; no one in fact had received the new entrant and introduced him to his new environment.*

Reception and Practical Instruction

Thus if we want efficiency, safety, and good discipline, in the sense of the adoption of approved procedures, it is vital that we do something about reception and practical instruction: not because any notable authority says so, not because we like people, but because people form habits. Anyone who has tried to drive a car with a gear change significantly different from his own will soon see what a handicap the wrong set of habits can be, and at the same time realize how much we rely on the appropriate habits to relieve us of the responsibility of attending to routine activities, thereby freeing us to make more important decisions about avoiding, overtaking, and the like.

Similar confusion can be caused over driving on the left- and right-hand sides of the road as in this country and the Continent. Hence the importance of the reminders on the roads near the Channel Ports.

It can be argued then, that the personnel functions of reception and practical instruction are based firmly on the foundations of habit formation—and so it is reasonable to ask: What are you doing about it?

Of course there is another byproduct of good reception.

People will feel that they matter—"This is a good place; they bother about you"—*the morale is right*. Thus a good reception and induction programme can help achieve efficiency, safety, good discipline (in the sense of approved use of facilities), and high morale. I do not know any firm which does not want these, but I know very few firms with a good reception programme.

Theoretical Instruction

So far this analysis has made the case for reception and practical instruction—for rule-of-thumb procedures—for habits. It has made no case for theory. What is the case for theoretical instruction?

People working on experimental and development work have on many occasions to do jobs which have never been done before. No one can teach them rule-of-thumb procedures for such work and, in fact, they have to work out procedures for someone else. In order to decide on a method for a new job they have to go back to theory as to how materials behave when they are treated a certain way and on the basis of this theory work out a procedure which is both efficient and safe. There is, then, no doubt about the case for theory for a person concerned with experimental and development work, but is there a case for theory for all people? I believe there is, as the following example shows.

At one time we used to fill a bullet as follows: We had a scoop which held $2\frac{1}{2}$ grains of powder when full and this powder was loaded through a funnel into the bullet envelope. The powder was then pressed on a hand press at 150 lb deadload. The increment was then repeated. Now the tool used for the pressing was a loose fit and so some of the powder crept up the side as "upstand". This we scraped out to leave a clean surface on which we put a couple of sealing components. The envelope was then closed on a press and boat-tailed at the end, resulting in the completed bullet.

This design was worked out by Design Department, Research Department, and Experimental Department in collaboration. The problem was now to get it filled in very large quantities by production.

In order to do this we met the overlookers (supervisors) in the shops and said: "This is what you have to do:*

> *Scoop* 2½ grains of powder.
> *Press* at 150 lb deadload.
> *Scoop* 2½ grains of powder.
> *Press* at 150 lb deadload.
> *Clean* off the upstand (dirt).
> *Close*."

This was given as a rule-of-thumb procedure presented orally—*oral communication*.

The first problem we anticipated was that some would forget—did he say 2½ or 3½?, etc., and so we wrote it down. We gave them a *written communication*.

Again we realized that some people did not like reading but preferred a pictorial presentation and so we gave them a visual aid—*visual communication*.

With this three-point attack we thought we had made a good job of presenting this rule-of-thumb procedure, anticipating several communication difficulties, but we had made a mistake—we had missed something out and, what is more, we did not know.

After a short time we found certain shops showing very high bullet production figures which were quite out of line with our expectations. About the same time we had reports from the ranges that certain bullets were not functioning when fired against appropriate targets, and, furthermore, that the badly functioning bullets came from the shops showing high production figures. Accordingly we put someone into the shops to find out what was going on.

What we found was that someone had said, "2½ and 2½ makes 5; what we really want is a big scoop". So they had one made and put all the powder into the bullet envelope in one filling. This saved one complete increment. They were proud of this: "Practical

---

* The situation is real but the figures are fictitious.

men we are—want any more advice? Come and see us in future!"

Now what was wrong? The answer is that they did not know that if a powder is pressed in a confined space it does not transmit the pressure. If a liquid is pressed in a tube it will transmit the pressure, as in hydraulics; but a powder will not. The granules resist, and a bridging operation occurs which supports quite a lot of the pressing load. It is not possible to press an infinitely long column of material in a confined space to achieve the kind of consolidation necessary for correct functioning.

We folk in the Experimental Department working with the Design Department had worked out the minimum number of increments (i.e. 2) required to give the right kind of consolidation in the nose of the bullet so that when it hit the target it went off. But we kept the reason to ourselves. We had given the overlookers the correct procedure but we had not given them *the reason* for the procedure and because we failed to do this we lost very considerable sums of money in reject ammunition.

It is necessary to work on the assumption that the listener will say of your communication, "What he means is this". He will alter your words more to his own way of thinking and he will add a little of himself in the process. He must be told *why* he must must perpetuate the key points. (It is not necessary to give a long talk—a technical paper—but sometimes only 30 sec work at the most, e.g. two increments to get the right kind of packing in the nose of the bullet for it to go off when it hits the target.)

Generalizing a little from these examples it can be seen that theory needs to be adjusted to suit the circumstances. The more a person is concerned with *novel* situations, the more he will need his theory, and the more he is concerned with routine situations the less he will need his theory. But everyone needs *some* theory to help him to co-operate intelligently with us in a situation for which we have no set procedure.

The case is made, then, for the importance of the personnel functions of reception, induction, and practical instruction and for appropriate theoretical instruction. This case is made largely on the grounds of habit formation and its consequences. Twenty years ago this was the kind of argument which we offered to justify these personnel functions, often in the face of counter arguments and views (the Personnel Officer as Parasite No. 1 the Training Officer as Parasite No. 2) which regarded these as luxuries and as devices to appease labour in conditions of full employment. But, of course, today we have the Industrial Training Act of 1964 which, via its levy–grant system, is backing the case for systematic induction and training. The danger is that training will be undertaken to ensure the return of the levy and the form of training adjusted to meet the approval of the appropriate training board as distinct from the needs of the firm. It behoves everyone concerned to see that the recommendations of the Training Board and the needs of the firm are not incompatible and that the activities of training board staffs and training departments of firms, both in day-to-day procedures and research activities, be directed to this end.

How Achieved

If at this stage of our analysis of behaviour we accept these personnel functions of reception and training, then the next question to answer is: How do we do it?

Reception and Induction

The first problem is that of personnel making contact with the new work situation.

Reception

Some years ago I arranged with a works director to speak to a group of foremen at his works at 3.30 p.m. on a particular day. As I approached the factory on the main road I realized that I did not know where to go. The subject and the time had been fixed, but only the works for the place. When, however, I reached the main gates, I saw that someone had partly anticipated my problem because on the gates were two notices, one labelled "Visitors" and the other "Lorries". The "Visitors" notice pointed to the front door of the firm and so it looked as though the front door in this firm was regularly used. (I used to work in a factory of 23,000 people where the front door was never used except on state occasions—we always went round the back somewhere—so you can see my dilemma.) I got out of my car and walked up the steps into the vestibule of the building, carrying my large bag of charts. The Commissionaire, without asking my business but seeing my load, said: "It's not here Sir. It's round the corner." (A fellow with a big bag like that can't come in this way.) Interested to see what happened I backed out and set out along the perimeter fence to find this corner. On the way I came to a police box set into the railings with a policeman standing outside. I was just about to say something when the officer anticipated my problem and said: "It isn't here, chum. It's round the corner." Now I didn't know what *it* was, but guessed there must be something round the corner, and so I proceeded until I turned the corner to find the Time Office. After some delay they found the man I wanted. This was my reception.

On another occasion I had an appointment to meet an official in the vestibule of the main building of a firm at 2.30 p.m., but on approaching the Commissionaire found that he was not at all sure that he could bring the fellow all that distance to see me. It is on occasions such as these that I wonder if my concept of a commissionaire is correct. It seems to suggest a training need for one of us.

A Few Well-placed Labels

Continuing aids to reception, I once found myself in the main offices of a large undertaking and discovered the doors were numbered 1–500 and that was all. Now I defy anyone to remember the changes which are likely to take place in a building of this kind over a short period of time, and so can anticipate a good game of hide and seek occupying very valuable time. Why don't we put a simple label on the door saying who is inside and naming his job, and if you like, a phrase "Knock and stay out" or "Knock and come in", whichever you prefer, and when he leaves, unscrew it and take it to screw on his next door?

But let us look at a place where this had been done.

At one time I wanted to see the Registrar's Secretary in a university and so I found the place where the department was located by reading the labels on the doors. I came to two doors side by side, one of which said "Registrar" and the one adjacent "Private".

Now what's your guess?

Mine was that I had to enter the door marked "Registrar" to find his secretary and expected that the Registrar himself would be in the room marked "Private".

Accordingly I opened the door marked "Registrar" and walked in, and there he was—the label was right; the Registrar was in the room marked "Registrar" and I had to go into the room marked "Private" to see his Private Secretary.

Again, I know a technical college in this country which says on its front door "Staff and visitors only". The people for whom the place was built cannot go in the front door they have to go somewhere round the back—not prescribed. If, however, you enter the front door you will finish up in the Administration Block which is not where the student wants to be. But the front door does not say, "This way to the Administration Block", with additional signals showing the way to laboratories, classrooms, and workshops; it in effect says to its most important clients, "Keep out", and almost "Guess how you get in".

Now this is all friendly chiding and it is not meant to be clever— it is easy to criticize—but it does illustrate the fact that the first aid which a newcomer wants on entering a place is a few well-placed, clearly labelled instructions, so that he gets to the place of work without undue confusion or excessive waste of other people's time. A notice which says to a lorry driver on a very busy road "No entry for commercial vehicles" is infuriating, but a notice which gives a clear positive instruction as to where to go "Commercial vehicles this way →" is very welcome indeed.

Induction

The question of induction procedures as distinct from reception is a much more extensive and exacting task. Induction is concerned with settling the individual into the new social setting of the work. He needs to know, amongst other things, the relationships of himself to other people in the department and the relationship of other departments to his. (Line management, trade unions, and functional departments.) He needs to know his contribution to the work of his department, the nature of the contribution of his department to the products of the firm, and the impact of his firm on the wider community outside. Later still he will need to know the state of prosperity of the community at large. The chart, Fig. 1, suggests a device for collecting information about relationships and communication problems which can be used to decide the content of induction procedures, but briefly we cannot hope for a person to identify himself with the purpose of an organization unless he knows what part he plays in the set-up, how he communicates in the set-up—in fact how "he matters" in the organization.

This need for some form of induction procedure applies to all cases of promotion as well as new appointments. There are some relationship problems to be clarified and catered for.

It is very encouraging to see the importance which some training boards are attributing to evidence of adequate induction procedures for grant purposes.

Training

It is obvious that a complete book could be devoted to the problem of training (indeed, it is surprising how much of the considerable research work by educationalists on teaching and learning has been ignored by industrial training), but for the purpose of this chapter some of the salient problems will be

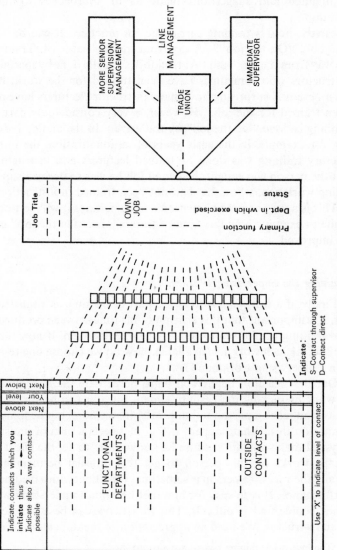

FIG. 1. Relationships and channels of communications.

highlighted and suggestions made as to approaches to their solution.

Firstly, how is training carried out in practice? It can be "At the job", "On the job", "Away from the job" at least. Training "Away from the job" and "At the job" is usually done by specialist instructors who sometimes have been trained for the work, but even here it is surprising how many instructors/lecturers have not been trained for the job.* However, a very considerable part of training is done "On the job" by tradesmen. In the mining industry, for example, in the early years of nationalization, the introductory training was done by trained lecturers and instructors, but the person was taught the actual job he was to do by a supervising workman, who often had not been trained in instruction.†

This is a very common situation and so perhaps it will be worth while to examine how this kind of training, i.e. "On the job" can be improved.

Training the Supervising Workman

Firstly, if a workman is to spend part of his time as an instructor, it is important that this sharing of his time between producing and training be allowed for on any payment system. If now there are several such workmen available, how do we choose one to act as a "supervising workman"?

Our first reaction might well be to perpetuate the best quality of work by picking the best craftsman. But this can be wrong. A coach can teach a person to jump 7 ft 1 in. or more, but he himself cannot do this. What happens is that he selects a man of unusual physical make-up and, because he knows how to get the effect he wants, works on this person to get this unusual performance. Again, the very able person is sometimes impatient with a mediocre performance. It is so easy for him that he cannot understand why other people find it difficult. This impatience can be a handicap in an instructor. We need an appreciation of the difficulties of the

* The industrial training boards are alive to this.
† This position is now improved, especially in the north-east.

beginner and some sympathy with the learner in face of these difficulties.

Thus we need to select a workman who is reasonably sympathetic with the learner and who understands what is involved. If he is a good workman all the better, because he can set good models for performance—but this is the second criterion and not the first. What I am saying is that it does not follow that a person must be able to do a job well in order to teach someone else. He needs to know what is involved and how to get certain effects, and above all, he needs to be tolerant.

T.W.I.—J.I.

Having selected our supervising workman how now can we help him to instruct? This problem was looked into in the early 1940's in some detail, when Perkins went over to America to look at the methods of rapid training of semi-skilled workers. Together with the Ministry of Labour, a scheme called T.W.I.—J.I. (Training within Industry—Job Instruction) was produced. This scheme provided a short training course on instruction, which was "sold" very successfully in this country and resulted in the formation of T.W.I. associations with the intention of improving the thinking about training and its practice in the country.

The early T.W.I. schemes were over-rigid and rather underestimated the interactive nature of all teaching. However, a great deal of very useful work was done, and I would like to suggest three things from the T.W.I. programmes which I think are invaluable in training any instructor.

Job breakdown sheets. The first aid to good instruction is the job breakdown sheet. Encourage the supervising workman to take a sheet of paper and rule a line down the middle. Now on the left-hand side of this line get him to write down the main parts of the tasks which have to be completed in order to do the job. On the right-hand side ask him to put the important points the operator should remember when he is carrying out these particular parts of the task. These should be tips or knacks (e.g.

pick it up with your left hand rather than your right), safety points, and bits of theory which might help. If a job breakdown sheet of this kind is completed, then instruction will improve considerably because *we are ensuring that the workman does some preparation before instructing.* It does not matter to me how experienced he is; unless he thinks out a plan before he meets an individual or group he will omit something and will regret it afterwards, resulting in wasted time. Now some people complain that this written breakdown sheet is difficult to achieve in practice. In these circumstances encourage a breakdown orally by asking the workman informally "Tell me what you propose to do". The T.W.I.—J.I. programme made a very good job of this work, and Fig. 2 illustrates the job breakdown sheet.

Training manuals. Some organizations were well convinced of the value of job breakdown sheets and went further to produce training manuals. The Coal Board did this for basic mining operations.* Very experienced people sat round the table and battered out a scheme for the most efficient and safe methods for selected operations. But, as Mr. Voysey, Publications Officer of the Young Farmers' Club Movement, has said many a time, "They had all the fun". These experienced men clarified their own thinking about the procedures, but it is the supervising workman who should do this. For this reason I believe it to be vital that the individual supervising workman should do this job breakdown for himself: he must agree, via a discovery method, that this is the best solution. Accordingly I suggest the following procedure: The supervising workman should attempt a job breakdown for himself. He should then match his breakdown with the approved solution in the manual and discuss any differences. Often the supervising workman will need to change his own scheme—but he will now know why. Occasionally the training manual can benefit from a new look and learn from the supervising workman.

For example, I remember one situation where a girl was able to eliminate one complete operation by discovering that a cementing bristle could be held in the *back of the hand between the fingers* and

* Published by Recruitment and Training Branch, 1951.

Important steps in the operations	Important points to be observed

In the Ministry of Labour's T.W.I.—J.I. programme these two columns are described as:

A logical portion of the operation which substantially advances the work.	Anything in a step that might: Make or scrap the work. Injure the worker. Make the work easier to do, i.e. "knack", "trick", special timing, bit of special information.

FIG. 2. Sample sheet for breakdown of operations.

so release the finger tips for movement, instead of holding the bristle *in the finger tips, in front of the hand* thus immobilizing the fingers. (Try it—she had no need to return to the cementing bristle to the pot of cement before engaging in the assembly operation concerned. She kept it between her fingers at the back of her hand all the time.)

Breakdowns and safety. This same procedure can be adopted where it is important that specified procedures must be adopted in the interests of safety. *Involve the individuals in decision making about the procedures,* i.e. invite them to work out their own procedure—compare this solution with the approved procedure—discuss differences.

Give credit where due. The second important point for the supervising workman is illustrated by a procedure worked out by some staff trainers in the Nuneaton Staff College of the mining industry. Some twenty instructors in training would be taken underground to practise instruction on a "training face". The night before, one course member would be designated "instructor" a second "trainee", and a third "supervisor". The instructor would do a job breakdown of a basic operation of, say, "Setting a prop to support the roof". He would check this against any source of authority available. The next morning the group would go underground. The three selected would go forward to the workplace and the rest would crouch down on their haunches as observers.

The instructor would demonstrate the task to the trainee, who would in turn attempt the task. Then the supervisor would critically examine the work of both the instructor and the trainee.

The key words are "critically examine". A number of people think they should always find fault and never applaud. But we need to know when we are right as well as when we are wrong. We need to know what to *perpetuate* and what to *alter*. Thus the words "critically examine" should read "evaluate", and we can well adopt the T.W.I. phrase (job relations programme) "Give credit where due". Tell him where he is right and tell him where he is wrong.

In the above training system the work did not stop there; the tutor in charge of the group then required *all observers* to comment on the work of one of the instructor, trainee, or supervisor, and in this way all twenty were involved. Those not engaged practically were given the task of observing, and this was checked.

Roles were then switched and the complete session would include several such demonstrations and evaluations. The general effect of this method was considerable, especially as it dealt with "real" operations as near the actual working environment as possible.

Training timetable. The third thing I would like to emphasize is the importance of a training timetable.

Entrants for training do not necessarily arrive in neat groups, but often at staggered intervals. For this reason a training timetable is an asset in that it:

(a) Reduces pressure on memory.
(b) Provides a guarantee of continual progression and overlooking.
(c) Provides a convenient device for recording performance levels.

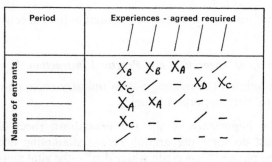

FIG. 3.

Figure 3 suggests a simple minimum scheme.

First along the top edge we should write the experiences considered essential in the training of that class of labour. These should be agreed with the persons likely to supervise the entrant before they are asked to undertake such supervision, i.e. in group discussion (or committee) at the planning stage. This means that when the time comes to ask for such supervision of training there is likely to be less resistance to the extra duties. (They are not really *extra* because some supervision of trainees must be undertaken either deliberately, or informally by all management/ supervision.)

Down the vertical axis list the names of the new entrants as they come in. The recording now consists of entering an oblique stroke, thus (/), on allocation to an activity and a cancellation, thus (X), when completed. If on completion of the training period a five-point rating A–E is allocated for general performance level (compared with general impression of that kind of labour—not very experienced or skilled men), then we will know four things from our record:

(a) Activities completed   X
(b) Where working at the moment   /
(c) Activities still to do   blank
(d) General run of performance   (A–E)

All this information is useful and minimum time is consumed.

Relationship of Theoretical and Practical Instruction

In my opinion the training within industry programme establishes three very important things:

(a) The importance of the job breakdown sheet—everyone must do some preparation before attempting instruction.
(b) The phrase "Give credit where due"—the vital motivational element.
(c) The value of the training timetable.

Readers who have participated in the T.W.I.—J.I. programme will probably also want to see an emphasis on the *four-step method of practical instruction,*

i.e. instruction where the object is for the learner to *reproduce what the instructor demonstrates.*

The formal steps of the T.W.I. scheme are:

(1) Prepare the worker—*preparation* stage.
(2) Present the operation—*presentation* stage.
(3) Try out the performance—*application* stage.
(4) Follow up—*consolidation* stage.

Involvement in such formal steps of instruction, however, runs us into difficulties when "theory" gets involved with the practical rule-of-thumb procedures. This is illustrated if we look at the steps of *theoretical instruction* in contrast to practical instruction.

The first two stages of preparation and presentation are involved, but the third stage is not one of reproducing what was demonstrated, but is one of abstracting a principle from what was demonstrated in order to employ this in a *new situation, which is different.*

The routine looks more like:

(1) Preparation.
(2) Presentation.
(3) . . . . abstraction.
(4) . . . . application (new situation).
(5) . . . . consolidation (other situations).

A good example of this is the T.W.I.—J.I. method of training the trainers.

The course members practise small training exercises, e.g. tying unusual knots, putting flints into lighters, etc., where a four-step method of practical instruction is emphasized. But we hope the course members will emerge from the training session having made the abstraction—four-step method of instruction—and *not having learnt to reproduce ten different tasks,* e.g. tying knots, putting flints into lighters, and so on.

Now it might be argued that, in the above, the course members were undergoing theoretical instruction, but my point is that in all practical instruction, as soon as an element of skill is involved, so some theory (however practical) is automatically involved, and in no situation, however prescribed it might be, i.e. however routine it may be, has theory been eliminated. The bullet example earlier in this chapter illustrates how important this is.

Herbart* looked at formal steps of instruction as early as 1800; and training schemes in the Services in the First World War enphasized four steps, but the rapid switching from practical to theoretical instruction involved in all teaching–learning situations suggests that the steps should be regarded as broad areas of emphasis rather than precise and limited stages.

The points made on both sides of the T.W.I. job instruction card—"How to get ready to instruct" and "How to instruct"—are invaluable, but they are useless unless they can be transferred to a new work situation. Thus it is futile to be word perfect on the content, i.e. achieve exact recall, without appreciating how these ideas can be employed in a new situation, i.e. appreciate the possibilities of transfer.

I am reminded of F. C. Bartlett's statement, "Exact recall is very rarely of any use."

Finally, in this pursuit of industrial training let us not forget *motivation*. Training needs are not just skill and knowledge—they are for

skill, knowledge, and attitude.

A Brief Note on Awareness of the Training Function in Supervision

On several occasions when dealing with groups of foremen on the question of the implications of habit formation for training, I have had the reaction, "Oh, very interesting, but we don't do any training." My retort is, "Supposing I joined your firm on Monday, what would you do with me—would you send me on a course somewhere before I could start working?" The reply is usually something to the effect of, "Oh, no! I would put you with Bill X

* See Adams, *Exposition and Illustration in Teaching*, MacMillan, 1929, J. F. Herbart (1776–1841), (ch. xi, pp. 143–5).

and ask him to look after you and show you." And immediately they realize they have a training function—not necessarily one of instruction, but of programming and overlooking. Taking this further it is obvious that every supervisor/manager is continually assessing individuals and the demands of jobs, is constantly involved in placement, and in this activity is actually engaged in extending the individual and is thereby actually involved in training.

Courses for supervisors can bring about an awareness of this situation and help the cause of training in this way.

Reflex Actions

This section on habits and training cannot really be left without some mention of reflex actions. At one time operatives working in a particular department were measuring a fine powder by weighing out increments on chemical balances. The fine powder tended to fly in the air and resulted in a good deal of sneezing. The sneezing made accurate weighing difficult and powder was scattered all over the balances in a very untidy state. Now it was no use blaming the operators for this state of affairs. They were healthy animals who sneezed when the powder irritated their noses. The only thing to do was to provide masks to prevent the dust from setting up irritation and thereby ensure accurate weighing and clean balances.

There are obviously a whole range of built-in reflexes which are very little under our control, except in arrears (we can control the extent of the splutter after a sneeze, or, if we know in advance, we can hold a hot plate), but other reflexes such as the dilation of the pupil of the eye, are so little amenable to training that we have to admit that "glare" will always be a problem in the sense that we find it difficult to dilate or contract the pupil of the eye at will.

It seems, then, that for a whole range of reflex actions we have to accept their existence—do little about training—but avoid the circumstances which call them into operation by the employment of eye-shields, masks, and protective devices of appropriate kinds.

CHAPTER 3

Motivation—The Background to Incentives

Incentive—Material Gain?

The word "incentive" today is used in such a way that almost invariably it implies material gain. The work study engineer talking about incentive systems is thinking of financial incentive systems; and a well-known group some time ago gave away £250,000 to some of its executives with the statement "What they want is an incentive". So common is this usage that we have to ask ourselves: Is this the answer? Are people only motivated by material gain? It is true if you ask the man in the street why he works, often he will say: "For money, of course. It's work or starve." But if you ask the same person what he advises his son to do, it's "Look for a job with prospects", and he is not at all sure what "prospects" means either. Money is in this, but not just money—other things as well.

I remember a lorry driver, during the building of the M1, being asked about his job by a reporter. He said it was a good job. The reporter said, "You mean the money's good?" The driver said, "Yes, that's all right, but the job's good." Several times the reporter tried to limit his statement to money, but each time the man insisted that there were other things and, so much so, that for the time being he had the other things really in mind.

Many Motives

It is easy to establish with groups of people (as on courses) that there are certain things they will avoid doing, irrespective of the financial incentives being offered, e.g. jobs of low social status involving unpleasant physical working conditions. They will reject jobs for moral reasons and some will not offer themselves for certain positions because they feel inadequate in knowledge and experience.

Thus we must assume that motivation is complex and that we will not solve our industrial problems by employing one single slogan—*material gain*. The text which follows will reinforce this theme and asks, and tries to answer: What are we sure about in motivation?

Basic Needs

I. Need to Survive Physically

The first thing I am sure about is that the human being has to stay alive physically, and anything which affects this physical survival will rank high in importance for attention. The biologist studies all living organisms on the plan of: What activities does this organism pursue to maintain itself alive? What activities does it pursue to maintain the species?

Thus the first basic need in the human being is the need to survive physically.

How do we use this in practice?

First we pay people money and give them material rewards to enable them to stay alive, and if these are stopped or challenged in any way—as in unemployment—people react strongly. Accordingly this has been the common refuge of anyone faced with a motivation issue—raise the pay.

In 1946 the mining industry of Great Britain had below 700,000 men and it wanted 750,000 to make it work effectively, and so it set about some active recruitment. Wages and material rewards were improved considerably, approaching the top of the industrial scale, but the adverse effect of high accident rate and the incidence of industrial diseases such as pneumoconiosis and silicosis, arising from the dusty conditions of work, had a deterrent effect, and labour targets were not achieved. Lord Citrine, member of the Coal Board for Manpower and Welfare in the early days, stressed the importance of the stigma of dirt and accordingly forged ahead with pit-head bath provision. His object was that a person should leave a mine (not a pit—a pit is a hole in the ground—a mine is a modern industrial undertaking) looking as clean and tidy as if he had come from a light engineering or food-processing firm. But people balanced pay and material rewards against safety and conditions of work in this need to survive physically, and sometimes decided to look elsewhere. The mining industry still has recruitment problems (1967), even in its most successful regions, but, of course, it does not follow that all the reasons lie in the need to survive physically. But certainly pay and material rewards did not and have not solved it.

Paramount in this need to survive physically is the element of security of tenure. We hear people say in states of great exasperation, "What we want is a bit of healthy unemployment, that will bring people to their senses!" And my reply is, "Unemployment for whom—for you?" It is always unemployment for someone else. The implications are that a bit of healthy unemployment makes for greater efficiency in industry—but for other people—not for oneself. My guess is that there are no economists in the economist's postulation of a 3 per cent unemployment figure.

But is this theory that unemployment makes for greater efficiency true? What evidence is there to show that this is true? In my experience a threat of "healthy unemployment" has resulted in "healthy restrictive (protective) practices" (the word healthy depending on which side you were on).

Restrictive practices and insecurity

In 1932 after a long spell of unemployment, I got a temporary job for a month as a specification clerk. On my second day an urgent job developed and we were asked to come back to work to complete it. I lived near the firm and got back early and decided that, as the job had to be done, I had better start work. About 10 minutes later, when the other two persons returned, they blew me sky-high.

"What are you playing at? You're spoiling the job."

"What do you mean, spoiling the job? You want it doing, don't you?"

"Look here, chum, we know you are a stranger to this kind of work, but this is a good job. There's two million unemployed outside, so you stretch it."

Again I had a friend who was trained on heavy ordnance work. He said to the man who was training him,

"I can't understand what's in your book!"

"I don't intend you to", was the reply, "or otherwise you could do my job."

In contrast, however, during the war I found some operatives only too pleased to co-operate in our work study and, what is more, actually thinking of ideas to improve it for us. Insecurity here had gone.

But contrast this again, in the late 1950's. I was due to speak to a group of foremen in a firm and just before we started the works director said to the foremen: "Look, gentlemen, you will notice we have changed our policy about the amount of work standing about in process on the shop floor. You will not see as much work about as before, but because you cannot see the work standing about you have no right to assume we have not got the orders. And I say this to you because the efficiency of this factory has gone down in the last month."

To me this said—not so much work about to produce—stretch it—no redundancy, no four-day week. The efficiency of the factory had gone down when they couldn't see as much work about to produce.

I do not think there is any doubt about it; there is a direct link between restrictive practices and insecurity and so the real problems are: What do we gain from fear?, What do we lose by restriction?, and if the statements made about restrictive practices since the war make any sense at all, my belief is that we lose more by restriction.

Nevertheless, a sudden recession could call forth a sudden surge, as with temporary overtime, but when unemployment becomes a permanent feature of industrial relationships, as in the early 1930's, people will manœuvre with this in mind.

Unemployment—a temporary feature of industrial relations?

I believe that we cannot work out our management principles on the assumption that unemployment will be a permanent feature of our industrial relations,* and so we had better assume that unemployment will be a temporary feature of industrial relations and plan accordingly. We are not likely to be in a position to dispense jobs in the form of bounty (not even if we want to) but will be asking people to co-operate with us in a joint effort to produce. We cannot use fear, and so need to ask: Why should people co-operate with us in our venture?

The set of motivating devices grouped in the need to survive physically (see Fig. 4, p. 54)—all threaten a person's life in some way and could hardly be regarded as the motivating devices of an advanced industrial civilization. What then are the alternatives?

Security

Let us start with this term "security". This is the "link word" in discussing the alternatives. It has been suggested by some people that if individuals are secure they will not work. This kind of argument has been levelled at the Welfare State: "You're spoiling them, they (always someone else) won't bother!"

My reply has been to try to get groups of people to consider the proposition, "Would you agree to do nothing from tomorrow onwards if I guarantee your living in the world?", and I have had no "takers" except one man who said he would stay in bed. The different groups all realized they would do something (the man in bed would, sooner or later—especially when his heels got sore). They would all engage in some activity and would involve others

---

* But see later (p. 66) for additional comment on the word "unemployment". At the moment we are in a transitional stage where the above applies.

in it as observers and commentators. The following example illustrates this point.

A friend of mine grows chrysanthemums and he grows them very well. He sends for me most years and I go to see him for at least three very good reasons. First, he talks a lot of sense and we have a "good old natter" for about a couple of hours. But this does not go on all the time. After about 10 minutes he says, "Let's see what we've got down the garden." Now I know what is down the garden before we go, but still we go, and there they are, in the autumn, about 700 plants in bloom—a wonderful sight. Now suppose I look at these flowers and turn to walk back to the house without saying a word. What will happen? My friend will be dismayed. He may even find it necessary in his embarrassment to ask, "What do you think of them?" because he thinks he has done a good job but needs someone else to confirm this. He gets his idea of standards from what other people say. Accordingly, I applaud certain specimens but might question others. He does not mind if I criticize: he prefers me to applaud, but he can't stand this deathly silence, this state of no comment, "no evaluation".

Of course, the third reason is that when I leave there are a couple of bunches of chrysanthemums in the back of the car.

Now you might well say: "What's all this about? What does this signify?"

It means that we all have to do something. We have to express ourselves through some activity. We could not exist like a budgerigar in a cage. Hence the next basic need in the human being is the need to express oneself through some activity, with the additional requirement that the community comments on that activity, i.e.

The need to do something—well.

If you prefer, the "need to survive mentally", as well as physically, or as some would have it—the need to excel—the comments of the community recognizing this excellence.

II. Need to do Something—Well

Figure 4 on p. 54 lists some of the incentives which are linked with this need, but it might be worthwhile to point some of these.

Physical evidence of work done

In some tasks it is possible to see the physical evidence of work done—things piling up which we have made, or a pile reducing as processing proceeds. But in some cases we deny the person this satisfaction by removing the products of his labour, and so he gets substitute satisfaction from counting chalk marks he has entered on a wall to record what he has done. In some tasks it would be well nigh impossible to see physical evidence of work done except by, say, changes in expression and facial contortions, as in a lecture (hence look at your audience—if you dare!). Thus certain jobs tend to be frustrating in this sense, and consequently individuals are inclined to relax by engaging in practical activities at home where they can see what they have done. But even these activities require recognition and qualification from outside, as a homely example will demonstrate.

Some time ago I busied myself doing some crazy paving. I was well satisfied by its general appearance, but this was not enough. (It was only me thinking it was satisfactory.) My wife had not been out to see it and so I invited her to come and look. And what did she do? She toured the site dropping out strategic comments from time to time, which she knew I valued, because she knew if she did not encourage me this year I would not dig the garden next.

It is not quite like that, but there is a great deal of truth in the illustration. The most important point implied is that *we need tokens to recognize our performance above the average and every one of these tokens is an incentive.*

Motivation—largely cultural

But we are taught to value these tokens by the society in which we live, and thus a great deal of motivation is cultural in the sense that these values are taught by the culture. When you were born you did not know what to value, but you have been taught what to look for by the society in which you live. Some of these tokens are discussed below.

Words of praise. The first, I think, is "words of praise". But there are two widely held theories about this:

(a) One group says—criticize, find fault, never tell a fellow when he is right, tell him when he is wrong.
(b) The other says—tell him when he is right—and tell him when he is wrong—evaluate—or, to use the T.W.I. phrase, *give credit where due.*

Hence the dilemma—criticize (meaning find fault) or give credit where due. We will resolve this later, but for the moment "words of praise" is queried.

We have to admit that in the late 1960's, in what we claim as an advanced industrial society, we are still so little certain of our motivational management systems, that we still debate the value of words of praise and some prefer criticism to evaluation.

Public awards. The second well-known set of tokens appear about twice a year by the formal announcement of lists of O.B.E.s, M.B.E.s, knighthoods, and the like. These are deliberate public expressions of approval and recognition of excellence.

Status symbols. Again there are facilities like access to staff status and dining room facilties, payment by cheque, special uniform and markings on the uniforms, admission to the membership of professional bodies, apprenticeship schemes, and the like. I remember a lad working very hard indeed, not for money but for a brass star in his cub's cap, because that is what he valued at the time.

How taught? Now I suggested that these incentives (values) had been taught.

One way is through the cultural impact of the literature.

At home we have a series of story books written for children around the age of 7 years. They are about the animals associated with a farm called Blackberry Farm.* One of the books is about Postman Joe, a robin who takes messages and news to the various farm animals.

One day he is flying up the lane when a squirrel nips down from a tree in a state of alarm because she has seen a large, red animal breathing smoke go up the lane and turn into the farmyard. Will Postman Joe go up there and see what is going on?

Joe flies up to the farmyard and there he sees the farmer and his wife and two children standing by the side of a large, red tractor, looking very pleased with themselves. The boy comes across to the robin and says that this is a new animal come to help his father and they are all very pleased about it.

Joe finds the excitement infectious and thinks to himself, "Ernest Owl (the wiseman) ought to know about this", and so off he goes to tell the owl about the tractor.

But the owl says that, in view of the fact that the squirrel was very alarmed about it, may be the other animals would be frightened if it turned up in the field unexpectedly. It might be a good idea if Postman Joe would nip round and tell them.

Joe thinks, "This isn't a bad idea", and so he spends the rest of the day flying round to tell the other animals about the tractor and, feeling pretty tired, flies back to his old kettle, thinking, "Ernest Owl will be very pleased with me for doing this".

And this part of the story finishes something like this—true enough, late that night Ernest Owl flew down to Postman Joe and told him how pleased he was for the service he had rendered the other animals.

You should read the actual story, but at this stage you might well ask: What has this to do with me and the problem of Motivation? And this would be my answer: I don't know whether you

* With grateful thanks to the author and publishers of this series—Jane Pilgrim, Blackberry Farm Books, Brockhampton Press Ltd., Leicester.

have ever bought books for children of this age (7) to read, because if you have you realize they do not read them. You do! They engineer situations where you read the stories to them. They are just about to go to bed when they say, "Tell me a story, Dad", (more often Mum), and so out comes the book with a show of real, or feigned, exasperation. We attempt to collapse the time scale by omitting bits, only to be brought back by, "No! You've left out the piece about so and so."

Well, it was after one such session that I realized, suddenly, what I had been doing. In this comfortable, warm, ideal learning situation and by this method, I was actively teaching youngsters:

(a) that service to the community was to be valued;
(b) that they could look for words of praise from people held in high esteem (Ernest Owl); and
(c) that those people would take the trouble to come to tell them (Ernest Owl flew down to Postman Joe);

i.e. that service to the community was to be valued; that responsible people in that community would recognize a good job when they saw one, and would take the trouble to go to tell the individual concerned.

And so this is the answer to our early dilemma. We have all been taught to look for words of praise by this kind of device. The phrase "give credit where due" makes sense.

If you do not like this kind of incentive in the culture, then, of course, you should never let this kind of story appear in a book, on the T.V. screen, films, or in a comic strip, because as long as it is present in the culture it will have its consequences. We talk about brainwashing as though it is only practised for special occasions, but every culture brainwashes in this way, in perpetuating its values.

Incentives not necessarily
transferable from culture to culture

If motivation is largely cultural, in this sense, then it is no use going to America to copy American incentive devices in this country because the English way of life is not the American way of life. We can look at what happens elsewhere and wonder about possible transfer, but generally we have to work out our own solutions. It is no use taking Western incentives to the Near East and Far East. It depends what they value in the Near East and Far East. It is not what you yourself value. It is what the people you handle value and, of course, they may value something quite different.* And we can go further. We have been able to demonstrate that Leicester is not a single culture at all, but a patchwork of subcultures where different things are valued.† In some parts of Leicester we could interest girls in factory work, but in other parts it was shops and offices because they had been taught (by the subculture) that these were respectable activities. I know a town where there is a district known as "Brown boots and no breakfast", suggesting a subculture characteristic which many could match—but would scorn or ignore at their peril.

I have heard general managers, in course review sessions, laughing their heads off at the kind of motivational devices used in other countries. But it is dangerous to ignore these culturally accepted signalling devices. Rather we should regard them as *different from*, not inferior to, our own progress charts, gold arm bands, special uniform, and ceremonial devices.

What values shall we teach?

Thus the problem facing us is, What values shall we teach in a modern industrial society?, because, as Hitler's team knew, we can change the culture of the next generation by teaching the things we have decided to perpetuate.

There has been a tendency to teach "pay and material rewards". The work study engineer on the incentive side has subscribed to this, and it suits the sales engineer in promoting sales to imply that material possessions represent success. Thus the work study engineer and the sales engineer can agree, but the effect is to debunk skilled activity and skilled supervision.

---

* See Wilkins, *Occupational Psychology*, October 1949, p. 235.
† See research findings on Figs. 5 and 6 (pp. 58 and 59).

The foreman today (1967) can find himself in the position of earning less money than the people he supervises when overtime is worked, and is in an unsuccessful job in this sense. He complains and so I say, "Why don't you leave, then?" His reply is that there are other things which matter, and he is balancing up these non-financial and financial incentives. The skilled man wonders why he learnt a trade, but still likes to tell you he is a "skilled so-and-so really" when you find him working on less skilled work for material reasons.

Skill revalued

The important point emerging here is that in teaching material rewards we are debunking skill. I cannot see that a future industrial society can afford to debunk skill—skilled operation, skilled supervision—and so believe that we must back-pedal on financial incentives. My main reason for this argument is that material rewards focus attention on satisfactions to be achieved outside the work situation, but skill has no meaning unless we exercise it within the work situation. I believe we are going wrong. We have to teach satisfactions within the work situation, and consequently we need to revalue skill with all the devices, M.B.E.s, and the like which we have used in the past to achieve recognition.

III. Need to Feel I Matter

The need to excel uses the culture to emphasize individual excellence. The individual stands out in the society. He uses the society to point his excellence. But we can feel lonely on this pinnacle of success and so another basic need emerges—one where our contribution matters to society. In brief, the "need to feel I matter".

Under this heading in Fig. 4 (p. 54) I have listed Reception, Induction, Consultation.

Reception

If we wish to show a person that he matters, we receive him as though he matters. Now earlier in this book we have made the case for reception based on habit formation—efficient habits, safe habits, and those approved on grounds of discipline. Here is a fourth reason. If a person is received well, he feels he matters. "It isn't a bad firm; someone bothers about you." In other words, morale is right. As I said in the previous chapter, "I do not know of any firm who does not want efficiency, safety, good discipline, and high morale", and so it pays us to concern ourselves about a good reception programme.

Induction

Induction means showing a person the part he plays in the set-up, how he relates to other people and they to him. In the mining industry the introductory training for new entrant youths amounted to 16 weeks' full-time instruction, designed to show the newcomer the basic operations in the industry and their theoretical background. This was done so that the newcomer could co-operate intelligently with the other people in a difficult and dangerous industry. And, of course, at the same time it showed him how he mattered.

This last point is worth developing because it is true that a great many procedures, or activities, are introduced into social organizations for technological or organizational reasons and earn a dividend in the sense that people interpret these innovations as evidence that "they matter", e.g. the improved lighting can be installed so that people can see better, but they also feel better—"someone is concerned about our well being".

Consultation and motivation

Reception and induction are concerned with motivation in the early stages. How do we hold morale high in the later stages?

This is a matter of how we consult with people. There are two kinds of consultation—joint consultation and informal consultation. In the first we elect someone to represent us on a committee, but in the second we discuss with a person a matter which affects us both.

Now the essence of consultation is that someone listens to what we have to say, accepts our views, brings us in on decision making. Hence the lift in spirits. We feel "we matter" because our views are being taken into consideration. We cannot delegate this; we must experience it. And so joint consultation and informal consultation must be different.

In *joint consultation* I help to elect someone to represent me on a committee. He is taking part in the decision making. He is involved, but I can only appreciate that I am involved. Thus joint consultation is largely intellectual appreciaton of the fact that I am being consulted. In *informal consultation*, however, I am discussing with a person a matter which affects us both and is urgent; the timing is right and I am very much emotionally involved.

This difference might account for the difficulties of joint consultation especially in trying to get a common agenda for people with widely divergent interests. For these reasons I believe that joint consultation should be reserved for those occasions where an obvious common interest is involved—redundancy, change of shift working procedures, major changes in methods of work and the like. But informal consultation, because it adjusts almost by definition to the situation pertaining, is really the cement of human relations.

There is another reason why we must consult, and this is concerned with communication.

Consultation and tests of communication

If I give you an instruction and you repeat it to me, it does not follow that you understand it. But if you repeat it to me correctly but using your own words, I know you understand. Thus the test of communication is not repetition, but expression in own words. If I give you an instruction and you carry out an appropriate action, I know you have understood me, but I need to be there to see the action or its products. If I illustrate things to you from my experience and you illustrate them back to me from your experience, I know you have understood me, but if you merely repeat my illustration I don't know whether you understand me or not. Thus the test of communication is *expression in*

> *Own Words.*
> *Appropriate action.*
> *Own illustrations.*

In other words I need some feedback from you to me which I interpret as evidence of understanding.

If I am to get this feedback, *I cannot be aloof from the people I supervise. I must Consult.*

IV and V. Group Needs and Sex Needs

The next two basic needs I would postulate as group needs and sex needs. Biologically I can readily see the possibility of some built-in systems to see that we struggle to maintain ourselves alive and also to perpetuate the species. A sex need to me is obvious, but a group need, which is something like a herd instinct, has always seemed to me to be derived, almost in the sense that it "pays us" to associate together.

Layouts and isolation

Certainly industry is a social organization where people talk; and any attempt, either deliberate or by accident (in the sense of layout of machines and premises), to isolate people will result in individuals leaving their tasks to talk, a state of affairs which is sometimes illustrated by excessive use of toilets. Some processes are such that little satisfaction (or variety) has been left in the physical working conditions, and so a great deal of reliance is placed on the social contacts with a neighbouring worker. I believe that quite a few married women are back at work because the kitchen sink is lonely—we don't get much response from the taps and potatoes generally. Any attempt to isolate such people then, is almost certain to result in high labour turnover—irrespective of bright polished surroundings, elegant furniture, and floral displays.

Not many people can work on their own. In fact solitary confinement is a punishment. My policy is to deliberately design layout so that people can talk and then, if they exploit this opportunity, we can do something about it because we know that this social contact represents a basic need. If, however, we start by isolating people, we can do nothing if they infringe.

Welfare

People in industry are not sterile machines. They have personal and domestic problems. These problems are not left at home. They occupy some of the attention of people whilst working, and in this way act as a drain on useful energy. Welfare is concerned with those personal and domestic problems which interfere with the work situation. Welfare is not just a question of canteens and sports clubs. These are two examples of welfare which are employed when necessary. I know a firm where the canteen is quite small because people can get home easily. Feeding is not a domestic problem for them. But, on the other hand, I once worked in a large organization many miles from the nearest town. The Social Club there was a real asset and the people who ran the bar made a fortune becaue they dealt with a personal and domestic problem. But I have known a firm in a town build a social club and curse the labour force because they did not use it. Why should they if they are already fixed up elsewhere?

Sometimes welfare amounts to making a telephone call for a person to prevent his being off all morning; sometimes it amounts to advice on a legal document or return which is worrying the individual; sometimes it amounts to a bit of advice as to how a man can get help from a social service because his wife is in a real difficulty. Welfare is difficult. It amounts to a continuous search for those problems which are worrying the worker and acting as a drain on useful energy. It is always with us and rests firmly on the foundation that man is a social animal.

Sex needs

Some years ago I was speaking to the Institute of Personnel Management in the Midlands on a Friday night on the question of Selection of Executives (mixed audience—senior levels). At one stage of the lecture I wished to draw attention to the problem of sex needs and selection, and in order to do this said: "If you employ over-spectacular girls as secretaries to your heads of department, you can expect the business of the firm to be interrupted from time to time by a number of telephone calls which have nothing to do with the job." I got a short laugh from the audience; felt I had made my point and went on.

But, unbeknown to me, there was a reporter in the audience. He forgot my main points and picked up this last one. I did not know anything about this until on Saturday a Sunday newspaper reporter rang me up and said, "I understand you made one or two controversial statements in Nottingham on Friday night." I said, "So I did, but that wasn't one of them, that's a certainty." He then began to ask further questions which I thought to be serious and which I treated accordingly, until suddenly he said, "What's your Christian name?" I now knew I was being taken for a ride and clamped down. He was looking for something to "guy".

By that time, of course, I was too late, but this would not have mattered had not some of the reporters from the national press on Monday picked up these Sunday "extensions" and elaborated further on my simple statement on the Friday. Again this would not have mattered much except that on that Monday morning I started work on a new job. As I entered the building one of the administrators stopped me and said, "Hey! What have you been doing, look here!", and produced a set of spectacular cuttings. He said, "I haven't shown them to the girls in the office yet, but you wait till I do!"

So much for sex needs. No one employing mixed labour can afford to ignore this need. It will bring problems to the supervisor, some pleasant, some difficult—but problems there will be. I know the principal of a training college who said, "Thank God this is a mixed college". I know of students in single-sex colleges (male and female) who, in a survey about forms of training, said, "Keep the men (women) out of the college and the work, we'll meet them outside." Some girls prefer a male supervisor and some men dislike working under women. I know a woman supervisor who got excellent results from a mixed team by putting the men in the last stages of a continuous line sequence of operations. Flattered, they thought they were in key jobs; in fact they only did the last stages of a line process.

The Diagram (Fig. 4)

Looking down the chart (Fig. 4), which is an attempt to list economically a great many of the points made, we can see the wide range of financial (material) and non-financial incentives available to the supervisor/manager.

Pay and material rewards are there, of course—I have never denied this. They could easily be the most important things on occasions, but they will not be the only things. Safety, security, and conditions of work will also be there.

The individual will be looking for some form of recognition in terms he has been taught to value, and he will be angry if this does not materialize. This is probably the worst thing we do. We do not tell a person what we think, but on odd occasions, when the timing is often wrong, we go to some trouble. The reaction is sometimes, "Oh, yes, what's he after now!" In other words, suspicion and suspected motives. It seems to me that as we pass a person at work, if we like the job, we should say so. The worker has no clue to the supervisor's thinking unless he does, or says, something. If we use this natural reaction, the timing will be right, the intonation will be right, and the worker knows very clearly the genuine from the assumed.

In a recent research we found that out of 600 building* workers 50 per cent did a day's work and no one commented on it—Who are they pleasing?

* Newcastle-upon-Tyne, 1965, Research Project, The Nature of Work Specialization in the Construction Industry and its Bearing on Technical Education.

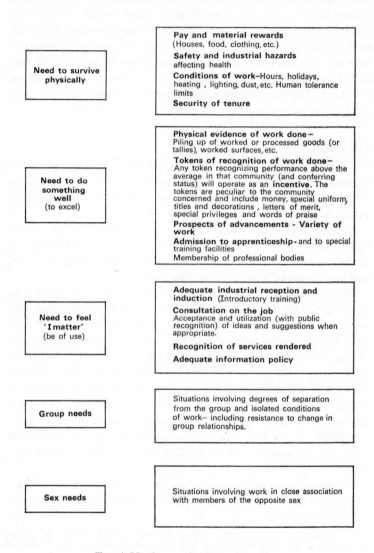

Need to survive physically

> **Pay and material rewards** (Houses, food, clothing, etc.)
>
> **Safety and industrial hazards** affecting health
>
> **Conditions of work**–Hours, holidays, heating , lighting, dust, etc. Human tolerance limits
>
> **Security of tenure**

Need to do something well (to excel)

> **Physical evidence of work done –** Piling up of worked or processed goods (or tallies), worked surfaces, etc.
>
> **Tokens of recognition of work done –** Any token recognizing performance above the average in that community (and conferring status) will operate as an **incentive.** The tokens are peculiar to the community concerned and include money, special uniform, titles and decorations , letters of merit, special privileges and words of praise
>
> **Prospects of advancements - Variety of work**
>
> **Admission to apprenticeship -** and to special training facilities
>
> Membership of professional bodies

Need to feel 'I matter' (be of use)

> **Adequate industrial reception and induction** (Introductory training)
>
> **Consultation on the job** Acceptance and utilization (with public recognition) of ideas and suggestions when appropriate.
>
> **Recognition of services rendered**
>
> **Adequate information policy**

Group needs

> Situations involving degrees of separation from the group and isolated conditions of work– including resistance to change in group relationships.

Sex needs

> Situations involving work in close association with members of the opposite sex

FIG. 4. Needs—motivations—incentives.

It is important to remember that in all our *normal life–learning situations*, applause (approval of performance) has been adjusted to the potentialities of the individual at the time. Thus we are delighted when the youngster (or backward child) recognizes simple words and Johnny Weismuller's coach used to "raise the bath" in applause when a young lad took his feet off the bottom of the swimming bath for the first time.

We have not transferred this attitude to our industrial incentive systems. *We have recognized performance and have failed to note that performance is a product of potential and effort.* We have rewarded performance and not necessarily effort. We have let potential smooth out some of the variance in *effort*. In judging when an incentive system is "fair", the individual will be concerned with *effort*, but the firm, as in job evaluation, will be likely to be thinking of *potential* and *later performance*, i.e. value to the firm. The acceptance of job evaluation in the industrial relations setting is likely to rest on the interpretation of what is "fair", i.e. effort and not what was innate.

Our "words of praise" systems need not suffer from this defect.

Moving further down the table, we note the importance of reception and induction as aids to high morale and especially single out informal consultation. A man in Ashington once said to me: "If you don't let me come in on decision making, don't blame me for anything which went wrong because you made all the decisions. But if you want me to accept some of the responsibility, then *you let me have a bit of a say, when I have a good idea which might help!*" I find this very hard to deny.

Finally, watch the way you isolate people either by accident or deliberately—man is a social animal—and, furthermore, if you employ mixed labour you will have pleasing and frustrating experiences which have their origin in the fact that we are members of opposite sexes.

Pressing the Wrong Buttons

Motivation, then, is a very complex problem and yet, despite its complexity, we managers, teachers, and supervisors—as

H.R.I.M.—C

psychologists—have learnt so much about people from our study of their behaviour that for the bulk of the time we press the right buttons and persuade people to work with us. But occasionally, we meet a case where we have gone wrong—the man is on strike— he refuses to co-operate—we have pressed the wrong buttons. What now should we do?

For a moment look at a parallel situation of a mechanical device which will not work. What action would we take here?

Well, of course, we could deal the machine a sharp blow in the hope that this would jar the bit straight. In fact, recently a scientist commenting on a projectile which had stopped functioning until it received a blow from some debris in space which triggered it off again, said, "It is surprising what a good clout can do to a transistor set."

But you would say, "This is clumsy." We prefer a man with a screwdriver, a spanner, and an oil can and, if he spends all day trying to find out what is wrong, we call him a good mechanic and we admire his tenacity of purpose in trying to solve the problem.

But if we return to our human being who refuses to work, our attitude is one of exasperation. He is defying us, and straight away we look for our big hammer—the most readily available sanction.

It pays us to adopt the policy of the good mechanic and try to find out what is wrong. The operative word is "pays", and the industrial training act will bring this home to many people.

It Pays us to find out What is Wrong

A foreman from a well-known firm told me some time ago that the firm had paid about £1000 on his training to date and he was only halfway through. An area official in another major industry told me that he estimated apprentice mechanics and electricians cost £3000 to train. A figure recently for sea-going engineers was £4000. An operative in a manufacturing industry costs £200 on training time, and I have heard estimates as high as £600 to recruit a graduate alone. If we think of sacking these people readily for their indiscretions, then we are being very free with the firm's money.

And so it "pays us" to try to find out what is wrong—and often we will. Nevertheless, in the course of our work we will sooner or later meet the abnormal kind of worker where, despite our efforts to find out what is wrong, we tend to fail. Then just as the mechanic will occasionally scrap a machine, so we will use our ultimate sanction and get rid of the individual. But, of course, the analogy stops there because someone has to deal with the person. Sometimes it is the courts, sometimes it is the mental hospitals, but society never escapes from the problem of trying to find out what is wrong with people who behave abnormally.

Research Findings

Over the last 10–15 years I have been able to collect research evidence on motivational problems from fair-sized groups of individuals. Some of these findings get "dated", but still illustrate important points. The diagrams appended summarize findings from:

(a) School-leavers in secondary modern schools (Figs. 5 and 6).
(b) Apprentices and young workers in industry (Fig. 7).
(c) Students in various departments of a technical college (Fig. 8).
(d) Building workers in the construction industry in the north-east (Fig. 9).

In the last case we correlated "satisfaction with the day's work" with other variables like, "working alone, recognition, faulty work, social communication, adverse working conditions, and outside events, and the evidence of correlation between the pairs of variables is surprising. When we realize, further, that in the work situation several of these variables would occur simultaneously in the experience of the individual, we see very clearly that

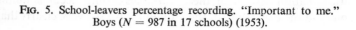

FIG. 5. School-leavers percentage recording. "Important to me."
Boys (*N* = 987 in 17 schools) (1953).

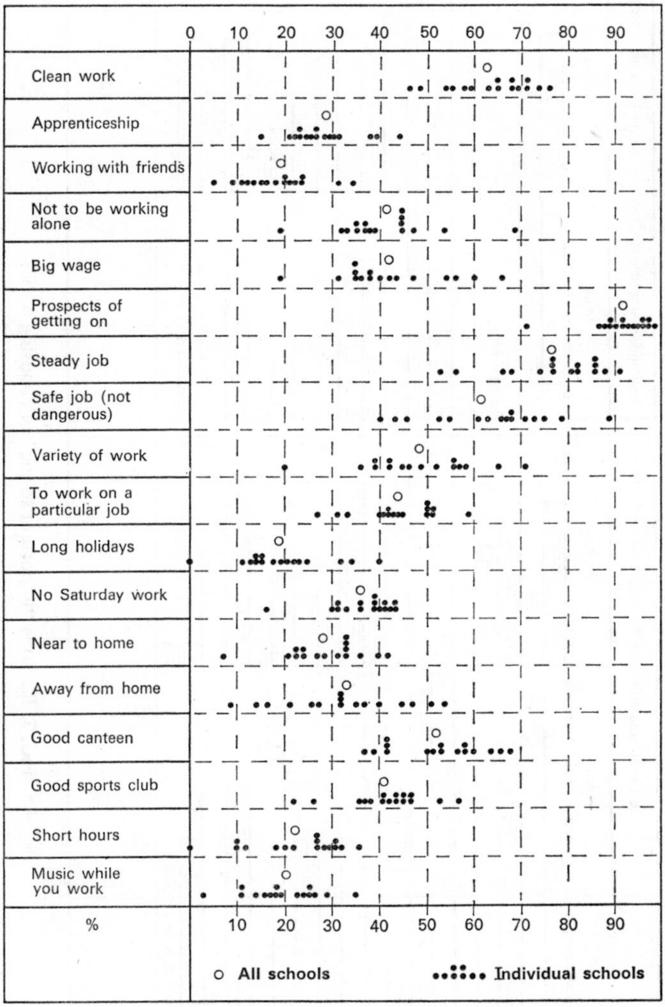

FIG. 6. School-leavers percentage recording. "Important to me."
Girls (*N* = 1071 in 16 schools).

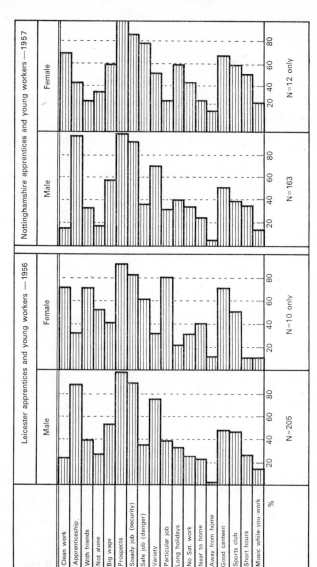

Fig. 7. Reasons "important to me" in choosing a job.

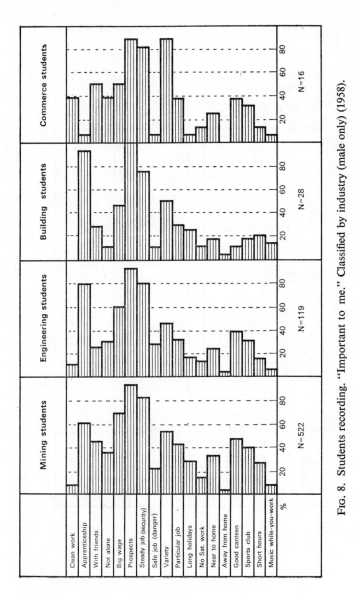

FIG. 8. Students recording. "Important to me." Classified by industry (male only) (1958).

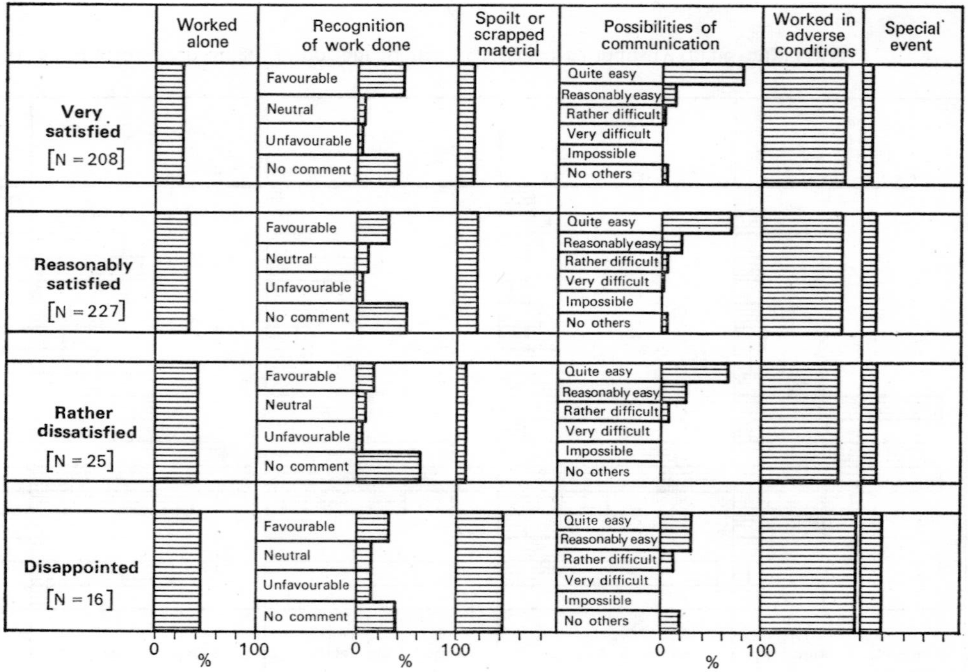

Fig. 9. Some human relationship factors abstracted for the five trades (1964): gas fitters; heating and ventilation engineers; plumbers; bricklayers; carpenters and joiners.

motivation is a question of a balance between a number of financial and non-financial incentive systems; the chief amongst the latter being

Recognition. Consultation. Communication.

In the case of the salaried worker it is the non-financial incentives which are paramount, but as more and more productivity agreements and new outlooks on payment minimize the effect of financial incentives, motivation will depend more and more on recognition, consultation, and communication.

We are never going to escape from the need to continually motivate people. Individuals will still want to excel and to feel they matter despite the fact that social legislation in the form of redundancy payments and the like and negotiated agreements with the unions will have minimized the impact of threats to physical survival.

The basic needs listed in Fig. 4 (p. 54) are possibly fundamental (see **Dr. C. M. Flemming** for further evidence* and postscript, p. 64) but their expositions are cultural. We can see physical survival and its associated incentive elements but, of course, we need also to survive mentally; hence, the expression through some activity and the need to excel. It seems as though we need some cultural device to point our excellence, and then, being isolated in our state of pre-eminence, need also to feel we matter to the society which has recognized our quality. Whether there is such a thing as a herd instinct I doubt if we will ever know, but at minimum, group needs ensure security and survival. Finally, sex needs are rational enough if we accept the biologist's view that we can study all living organisms on the plan:

(a) What activities does it pursue to maintain itself alive?

(b) What activities does it pursue to maintain the species?

Are there built-in "programmes" to see that this is done and are these the origin of our complex motivation systems?

* *Adolescence*, Routledge & Kegan Paul, 1948, (ch. v, pp. 44–49).

Figure 4 (p. 54) represents my attempt to structure these systems, and the preceding notes an attempt to justify the five basic needs. In the ultimate, however, the central theme is "survival", and so we can see how important it is for the individual that his work should *be recognized*, that he should *be informed* about the work situation, and that he should *be involved* in decision making about it.

Postscript

Most of the basic analysis work for the data of Fig. 4 was worked out in the early and mid 1950's mainly for overseas executive courses and for supervisory and management groups in both private and public sectors of industry.

The reader might like to refer to some of the papers published in this field of satisfactions and incentives in *Occupational Psychology*, for example, around this time:

Satisfactions in work, N. Balchin, **21** (3), July 1947.

Satisfactions in work, C. A. Mace, **22** (1), January 1948; **22** (2), April 1948.

Payment and incentives, C. Madge, **22** (1), January 1948.

Sociological background to incentives, A. Curle, **23** (1), January 1948.

Men, machines, and productivity, F. C. Bartlett, **22** (4), October, 1949.

Incentives and the young worker, L. T. Wilkins, **23** (4), October 1949.

Advances in the theory and practice of incentives, C. A. Mace, **24** (4), July 1950.

What is occupation success?—symposium, J. G. W. Davies, M. B. Stott, and J. W. Reeves, **24**, 1950.

Measuring motivation in industry, F. A. Heller, **26** (2), April 1952.

Raising job satisfaction, J. B. Handyside, **27** (3), April 1953.

Incentives, S. Shimmin, **29** (4), October 1955.

It is interesting now, some 10 or more years later, to see the case in American literature for:

MASLOW'S HIERARCHY OF NEEDS: A. Maslow, *Motivation and Personality*, New York, Harper, 1964;

HERZBERG'S HYGIENE FACTORS AND MOTIVATORS: Herzberg, Mausner, and Snyderman, *The Motivation to Work*, New York, Wiley, 1959;

ETZIONI'S ORGANIZATIONAL RELATIONSHIPS: A. Etzioni, *A Comparative Analysis of Complex Organizations*, The Free Press, Glencoe, Ill., 1961;

MCGREGOR'S THEORIES X AND Y: D. M. McGregor, *The Human Side of Enterprise*, New York, McGraw-Hill, 1960;

and their evidence for the supportive role of management in the motivational field.

Summary of Practical Conclusions

(1) Do not put all your eggs in the "pay" basket.

(2) Remember that people coming from different environments have been taught to value different things and all these things will act as incentives for those so taught.

(3) Remember also that we can change the motivation of the coming generations. What shall we teach? Material rewards or satisfactions to be achieved within the work/group situation.

(4) Remember the importance of reception and induction into any new activity. It pays you on grounds of efficiency, safety, good discipline, and morale.

(5) You cannot afford to be aloof from the labour you supervise (a) because informal consultation is the basis of high morale, (b) because the test of communication is expression in own words, actions, and illustrations. Feed back of information about reactions is vital as in any communication system.

(6) We can expect resistance to change. The attitudes we take up are multi-based and will not be changed by *one single logical appeal*. It will take time. Use (a) more discussion—so that people

find out for themselves, (b) long periods of notice in cases of redundancy (see Chapter 4).

The resistance is mainly located in the sentiments which we form—they make for stability but resist change. Our social engineering will always be in arrears of our technical engineering.

(7) Remember industry is a social organization. You are concerned with the personal and domestic problems of the labour you supervise.

(8) If you employ a mixed labour force (men and women) remember intellectual differences, in general, are slight but differences in interest are considerable. Occasionally the fact that they are members of the opposite sex will cause you trouble which you cannot ignore.

Multiple motivation, not *single motivation*, is the key to our difficulties and perhaps the origin of our satisfactions in supervision.

If a human being will not respond, he presents as great a problem as does a complicated machine which will not work. Both present a challenge to our skill as social and technical engineers. Both require the same degree of patience and ingenuity. Both represent potential sources of considerable satisfaction to the engineers.

Note on Unemployment

If automation and computer control makes any considerable impact on industry/commerce, the need for continuous operation will have considerable significance for shift working. Large productivity agreements have resulted in a diminution of the total labour force in firms, and the merging and shaking out of redundant processes, on the one hand, or in shorter shifts, on the other. Some of these redundancies have been resolved by early retirement, natural wastage, and small recruitment, but this cannot be relied on to go on indefinitely. It is really a "one off" policy, and so ultimately we shall reach the stage when we shall have as alternatives:

(1) a large number of small shifts so that everyone can do some work; or

(2) a limited number of people working and the rest not so occupied.

These "unemployed" (and the "workers" when at leisure) will, of course, not be inactive, and so it appears that we may have to choose between:

(a) activity using costly resources to develop one's own ideas, ultimately for the benefit of a larger group of people, e.g. aerospace design—now designated work activity; or

(b) activity using less costly resources to study for one's own or a limited number of people's benefit, e.g. Russian or music—now designated leisure activity.

Thus the word "unemployed" will have no real significance because all will be active.

Peculiarly enough, the further education system has almost by accident anticipated this situation by offering courses in subjects to be pursued for their own sake rather than technical/commercial reasons, both in the L.E.A. province and in the extension classes of the university.

This state of affairs will also have considerable significance for the size of, and attitudes towards, the so called unemployment benefits.

Recently, in an industrial relations course, a labour relations officer cited this example. He said that they had to de-man by two persons and they had in the group two men of 64 years of age. He told these two men that if they retired now, with the compensation available they would be better off than if they waited until they were 65. But both refused. They said they wanted to work. His question was, "What should I do?"

This points what is likely to be an urgent problem if productivity agreements escallate. It will be the problem of unemployment through good management and not through bad management. And, of course, the only answer is: What alternative activities are available to the two men (possibly now called leisure activities) which their compensation might help to provide? We do not necessarily die when we retire or are made redundant. We will be "active" and not "unemployed".

CHAPTER 4

Persuasion—The Problems of Attitude Change

Three Aspects of Persuasion

The next important subject in this approach to the analysis and structuring of experience is the problem of attitude change—the problem of persuasion—the achieving of a desired response from people.

We shall get the response we want from people if they accept our ideas, and so the first thing we ask ourselves as students of behaviour is. How do people accept ideas from others?

I think there are three ways: Firstly, the transfer of ideas from person to person without there being necessarily a logical argument—*suggestion*. Secondly, we can call on biases and prejudices originating in the *sentiments* formed from our earlier contacts with people and things and ideas. Thirdly, we can transfer ideas by *logical appeals*.

I. Suggestion

The best example of suggestion I know is the negative command. If I say to you, "Don't put your cigarette ends at the back of the radiators"—immediately you wonder where these radiators are. "My word! I never thought of that!" Instead I should use a positive command. "Put your cigarette ends in the ash trays" and leave you to find the radiators for yourself.

We can see the danger here when we call out, "Mind you don't drop it" to a youngster carrying a piece of valuable china across a hard floor, or when, in a state of anxiety, we shout, "Mind you don't fall" to the child who has climbed the ladder to the bed-room window during our tea-break in the periodic house-painting exercise.

For this reason it is obvious that positive commands are much better than negative commands, but there are occasions when negative commands are almost inescapable. It is interesting to see that on all such occasions the notices are prefaced traditionally by some short sharp positive comment. Danger. . . . Warning. . . . This might mean you. . . . You have been warned. . . . Or even ! . . . This halts the individual, so to speak, and reduces him to a state of readiness for what may well be a negative command.

Some accident-prevention work is now directed away from the negative approach because of this suggestion element.

We can now see that it is possible to transfer ideas from person to person without, necessarily, a logical argument; and it is useful to consider the use of a number of prestige elements which can aid such transfer.

Prestige Elements—Based on the Converse of a Truth

Age

The first prestige element is age. It is unwise to send a very young person to sell a difficult idea. The reason is that youth implies inexperience. For that reason the older person with furrows in his brow and the mark of years about his figure, tends to be treated much more seriously. This element of age turns on the converse of an accepted truth. If a person has had plenty of experience he will be getting on in years, and so I send an older person to imply he has plenty of experience in the field in question. He has plenty of experience admittedly, but not necessarily the kind we want.

The suggestion of age accounts for some of the difficulties which the younger supervisor finds in trying to get accepted. It is not necessarily a question of what he does or has done; it is a question of age. This age factor can, of course, be taken too far. If we send a person who is decrepit, they may think his ideas are antiquated as well.

Rank

If we want to have a conference opened successfully we have it opened by a rear admiral, an air vice-marshal, or a bishop— Why do we do this?

A person can earn high rank in his own walk of life by sheer merit, and he is allowed to talk at that level in a walk of life in which he has no experience. If he insists on asking for acceptance at a humble level in this "strange" walk of life, his statements, in fact, tend to be given the level of authority which he possesses in his own profession. That is, we let rank transfer from one situation to another. This means that high-ranking persons have to be very careful about what they say in another field of life in which they have little or no experience. When the Bishop of X recommends work study—"It's the bishop, you know!"

Again, the successful man in another walk of life is often used to advertise newspapers—"My paper!"—cigarettes, drinks, and the like.

In brief the high-ranking person will get away with it when you will not—but maybe you are the high-ranking person in your business.

Stature

If you want people to think you are important you really must have an office—a desk behind a door only as a last resort. Now in the design of this office the room should be long with a door at the far end in order to make people walk a long way. There should be carpet on the floor, not wooden blocks or lino, so that your visitors cannot hear themselves walk. You should assemble your heavy furniture (not contemporary) at the far end and sit firmly behind it. Glare at the people as they come in and if this does not embarrass them, carry on your table a neat notice which you turn towards them as they are about to speak. This notice says, "Be brief".

You might say, "How ridiculous can you be!" Nevertheless,

this is the technique of a well-known managing director who does this deliberately to enhance his stature. It is aimed at a "permission-to-speak, sir" attitude.

You may still resent the implications and reject the technique, but the fact remains that we are all influenced by the quality of the presentation of the premises. So much so that I recommend to you very seriously that if you want confidences from a person, never put a barrier between you and him. Interview with seats side by side, informally. If, however, you want to enhance your stature, interview over a desk. High tables, reserved seats, platforms—all are devices for enhancing the stature of individuals, and for this reason are avoided in staff training establishments where we respect the experiences of the course members and no one usually claims to be the authority.

I remember once being interviewed by the principal of a technical establishment in the north of England. He had an impressive room and in front of his immaculate desk (implying efficiency) he had a "sit-up-and-beg" chair. At the side of the desk was an easy chair. He said to me, "Sit down, will you", and I chose the upright chair. Immediately he said, "Oh, it's formal is it?" Implying— "Going to be difficult, are you?" Had I chosen the easy chair he would have been relaxed. (Actually I had lumbago and it was easier to get out of the upright chair. So it shows how easy it is to be wrong.)

So much for the enhancing of stature by the premises we build around ourselves.

But this can also apply to other forms of presentation, e.g. the written word. I have in my possession a very impressive, loose-leaf, multiple-ring file. It is in green leather, embossed "Buyers conference" and has my name in gold lettering at the foot. This was a hand-out for a week-end conference for buyers from a well-known group. It was the work of the Training and Education Officer of the group, selling industrial training and education to the buyers, using their own techniques of buying and selling:

Presentation—this is good

implying that the material inside was good and the conference excellent before it started.

If you jot down your ideas on the back of an envelope not everyone will treat them seriously—present them well.

Again, if you apologize when you speak, some people will think you do not know, whereas you may be facing reality and adopting a realistic, albeit humble, position in the face of the complexity and difficulty of the situation. Occasionally talk with a note of authority, even though you do not feel that sure.

Some years ago I was taking a series of lectures in a management diploma course and in that particular session found myself with some sales managers in the group. One night a very able course member came in just before the lecture started and said: "I am sorry I have not been able to do the set homework because I have been very busy this week on outside work, but last night I found myself in a hotel with a little time to spare and so I have roughed out an answer on this paper, which is all I could get. Will you have a look at it and if you think it is any good I will write it out decently for you." He then handed me a large foolscap envelope which had been opened out flat and on which he had mapped out his answer, in close writing, on each side. I read the material he had submitted, made pencil entries by way of comment, and awarded the conventional mark out of 10. It was well done. The next time I saw him I said, "You need not make a fair copy of that homework, just file it as it is."

Now an extraordinary thing happened. For some reason the external assessor sent for the homework scripts of the course members as part of his assessment. I had never experienced this before, but duly collected the scripts as required and dispatched them. But not all, there was one short—the answer on the back of the envelope.

I was rebuked by the assessor who wrote, "Why do you record marks for a student, when you cannot produce his work?" I, of course, did not reply. If I, or the student, had sent in that homework script, do you think it would have been accepted? Do you think I would have received another rebuke? Do you think the standard of the conduct of the course would have declined in the eyes of the assessor? Or do you think he would have had a "hearty laugh"?

What is your guess? Do you think that stature is important and can be enhanced by presentation?

Number

If you are in a minority you feel uncomfortable. If, for example, I take a vote on a proposition and 18 out of 20 vote for it, then the two voting against it have to feel very strongly about the matter to maintain their position.

Some years ago I wanted thirty-one establishments to take part in a research. I knew that some would but that others would be hesitant and need convincing, but anticipated that one man in particular would be antagonistic. I went to three or four people who I thought might be reasonably sympathetic and argued with them logically that they would get so-and-so and we would get this and that and, on the whole, the town would benefit (note the order of appeal). After a short discussion (separate interviews) they accepted. When I went to the fifth person I said: "Look, I have an interesting research project here which I think you will like the look of, and I have been to see so-and-so and so-and-so, etc., and they all think it is a good idea." I then started to argue logically with him about the matter as I had done with my early contacts. By this device I was putting greater pressure on the fifth person, i.e. the pressure of number as well as the logical argument I had used for my first contact. When I had 30 out of 31 on my side, I went to the most difficult person of the group and my main argument was "Can you see your way clear to complete the picture?" What I was really saying was, "Can you afford to be the only person missing?" He could not, and very reluctantly came in.

So much for the suggestion of number.

This is the technique of the large public meeting. The speaker makes a strong emotional appeal from the platform and hopes for calls from the audience and might even place individuals to ensure these. There is an emotional surge and a snowballing effect which, if unscrupulously directed, can result in destructive crowd action. The individuals do not know why they have engaged in the action. They have been taken away on the prestige of number.

The technique of "lobbying" has its foundation in this prestige of number. Committees rarely make decisions from flat. The sympathies of various members have been canvassed and the hope is—especially on crucial topics—that the person "sitting on the fence" will fall over on the side of those exhibiting solidarity by a good show of hands, or a murmur of approval.

Lobbying relies on the fact that you have to feel very strongly about something to stay in a minority.

Printed word

When I came out of the university in 1931 it was very difficult to get a job. I applied for a great number of jobs with little success. One day I met one of my old tutors and anxious to help he said, "How are you off for testimonials?"

I replied I had three.

"What do you do with them?"

"Well, if I can get them typed I do so, but otherwise I write them out by hand."

"Oh! You don't want to do that, you want to get them printed. It only costs £5 for 100!"

Now I was out of work and, furthermore, a draughtsman's salary in 1931 was £5 a week, I.C.I. used to start its chemists straight from the university at £250 a year and it was possible to start teaching in a secondary grammar school at £234 per annum, i.e. £5 a week was a good salary in 1931. This tutor was suggesting spending sums of this nature to get testimonials printed—on the assumption, of course, that my testimonials printed were better than my testimonials written by my hand—the same words.

But in these days, when everyone types letters, I like to get one hand written—a real signature, not a rubber stamp—personal attention. So true is this that some advertising firms have gone in for the hand-written letter—printed.

It is extraordinary how much power there is in the printed word. Such phrases as, "It's down here in black and white", "It's in this book", are sometimes presented as the final argument.

Reality of Suggestion

And so this is suggestion: I might occasionally have appeared to have been fooling—but I am seriously discussing a technique of persuasion, of advertising, if you like. I have seen dismay on people's faces in a lecture at what appear to be the devices of trickery and deceit. We are talking about techniques, not necessarily recommendations. These can be used for good or ill and, what is more, the more subtle the suggestion the more effective it will be.

Suggestion is one of McDougall's three powerful socializing forces:

> *Suggestion* being concerned with the transfer of *ideas*;
> *Imitation* being concerned with the transfer of *actions;* and
> *Sympathy* being concerned with the transfer of emotions.

We shall never get rid of them—they are operating all the time. T. P. Nunn* talks about mimesis—the tendency in the human being to take over and fall in line with the ideas, actions, and emotions of others without there necessarily being a logical reason for doing so.

A number of powerful firms in this country have been very jealous of their public image because this can sell by suggestion. If anything happens to tarnish this image, good solid work must be put in to regain the original position. I heard a lecturer say quite recently that Rolls-Royce were very courageous in Quality and Reliability Year when they admitted that they, too, had a quality and reliability problem. Rolls-Royce, the name which stood for the paragon of quality and reliability!

* T. P. Nunn, *Education—Its Data and First Principles*, Arnold, 1930, p. 138.

Use of Suggestion

If suggestion is such an important element in our relationships, how then should we use it in persuasion?

It cannot be a firm basis for persuasion because its foundations are on sand.

Looking at Fig. 10a, suggestion says:

The *older* man always knows.
The *high-ranking* person is a certainty.
These *exclusive establishments* represent real merit.
The *majority* is always right.
The *printed word* can never lie.

This is the might of suggestion.

But we know:

The old man may be only old in years.
The high-ranking person can be artificial.
This exclusive establishment can be deliberately designed to make you pay more money.
Major movements have come from minorities.
And we have all seen examples of distortion in the printed word.

What then shall we do?

I suggest that if you have a poor product or a poor idea to sell, then sell it by suggestion with all its advertising devices and clear out! Don't come back! Because when your clients have discovered the truth behind this façade, they will be actively resentful. Contra-suggestion will set in and they will reject even your good ideas. When I discover that the man behind his great desk has not much of an idea, then I doubt his set up; in fact I have contempt for it and suspect even his genuine contributions. If my presentation is once seen to be flamboyant, then suspicion creeps in and contra-suggestion may operate.

But mostly we want to stay. We are in this business for a career. Then we should sell our ideas/products on their logical worth and deliberately use suggestion to get a quicker response, "extra

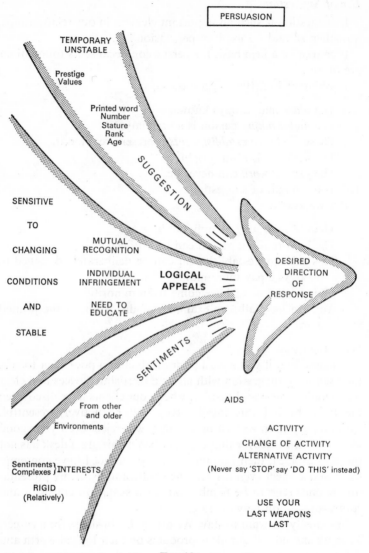

FIG. 10a.

weight in the pan", and then, when the effects of suggestion have faded, our clients will not mind, and may not even notice, because we have sold them something worth while in any case.

We should use suggestion to reinforce our more logical appeals and to get a quicker response.

Suggestion is frothy, spectacular, but ephemeral. It is an interesting exercise to trace the use of some of its prestige elements in everyday life and in modern advertising.

II. Sentiments

Sentiments have been defined as structures or organizations of emotions around ideas people or objects which tend to predispose us in favour of or against the idea person or object.

Let us look at this in a practical life situation.

I used to live in a cul-de-sac and opposite to me lived a dog. This dog did not like me for some reason or other and insisted on attacking me, nipping round my trouser legs and ankles. Now I do not like being charged in the rear unexpectedly. I prefer to move along the street with reasonable decorum and so I decided to do something about this dog.

My theory was that if the dog knew that I really was alarmed about his actions, he would become even more aggressive, and so I thought I had better pretend to the dog that I couldn't care less and in fact was the boss. So there was nothing for it, but a bit of suggestion of authority: the fact being just the reverse. And so I tried suggestion—the loud voice, the firm front—but for some reason or other the dog had never been taught any suggestion. He did not believe it—he saw through my scheme (or so it appeared to me—he might, of course, also have been trying to use suggestion—putting on a front) and he became even more aggressive.

I tried a new approach. I was wearing a soft cap, which I snatched off my head, suggesting a weapon (a soft cap as a weapon!). The sudden movement frightened the dog and he started to run and so I went after him. The faster he ran the bolder I got. I chased him up his garden path and shut the gate; pleased at last to show him I was boss.

But I was wrong, he thought this was a good idea and came to play this game every day. I would come down the road and get about 20 yards from this man's house and out would come my gloves ready for the onslaught—every day for about a month!

At the end of that time someone asked me what I thought of the dog. My reply was that it was a mongrel to start with, it was scruffy, and it was time it was shot because I hated the sight of it. I had developed a *sentiment of hatred*—not a single emotion but a structure of emotions. All my experiences had been unfortunate and I could not find anything good to say about the animal.

But what of the owner? He thought it was a nice dog. It wagged its tail when it saw him. He had plenty of pleasing experiences and had developed a *sentiment of liking*.

At this stage I decided this affair had to stop and so I went to talk to the man opposite about his dog. This was useless. It ended in worse confusion. Here we were trying to be logical about something which was emotional. He would never see my viewpoint because he had never had my experiences and I would never see his viewpoint because I had never had his experiences. We would only have a chance of rational agreement when we had *common* experiences, and I should have known better than to attempt it. We quarrelled and so I hated him as well as his dog.

This happens in mergers in firms. We build sentiments in relation to the separate firms and these result in attitudes like, "He's one of them" and, "He's all right, he's one of us". And this position will not change; it will stay "one of them", "one of us" until we have common experiences together. This affects all mergers—private enterprise, or public monopoly. The Coal Board, for example, attempted to merge 1000 undertakings—1000 major sentiments. Of course this needed time and opportunities for engineering common experiences.

Similarly, when the work study engineer or the O. & M. officer suggests a redistribution of labour, his logical arguments fall on deaf ears—"The labour force is pigheaded", he says, but the real trouble is the sentiments they have formed in relation to their present method of working. They are comfortable emotionally—why should they change? He is trying to tear the sentiments apart.

We can see the powerful effects of sentiments in mobility of labour. If I get a new job, for a short time I am on top of the world, but very soon the consequences of moving, affecting housing, schooling, relatives, public facilties, the local football team, the pub I drink in, and the like, all involve me and anchor me—resisting change. I have to build new sentiments, put down new roots in relation to my new environment before I have really made and completed the move. There is a trough of depression some two to three days after the successful interview when the consequences of having to rebuild new sentiments and sink new roots make themselves felt and consequently leave the individual vulnerable to alternative propositions designed to keep him in the old environment—to stay, in fact.

Sentiments, then, are our best friend if we stay as we are. They make for stability but they resist change. This is the origin of resistance to change.

Our national sentiments are our best friend in times of national emergency, but they are our worst enemy in international relationships where we are asking the same people to associate differently.

Some sentiments seem very resistant to change, especially those forged in the early years. The only sentiment I would deliberately foster is that which respects another human being. We only see it rarely when some natural disaster affects the lives of people and others come to help irrespective of creed, race, and colour. (This is a statement of opinion and I provide no evidence here to support it. The other events are actual observations of situations, illustrating the points I have made.)

Generally, then, sentiments are rigid. They are our best friend if we stay as we are but our worst enemy in times of change. They represent the chief origin of resistance to change.

III. Logical Appeals

The third element in persuasion we listed at the outset was logical appeals.

Mutual Recognition

We cannot argue logically about anything unless we have some premises on which to base our argument. Thus the first principle in logical appeals is "mutual recognition of relative responsibility". It is useless to complain of the failure of an individual to carry out a task or to exercise a function unless we have established at the outset that this was his responsibility. And yet we are very lax about establishing these terms of reference and agreeing objectives. Our researches with supervisors and management have shown considerable sensitivity to this problem.

But why establish terms of reference? Some people deliberately avoid it. My reason is very simple and it is this—the bulk of the people in this country—when they know what their tasks are—do them.

How do I know this?

In the first place a supervisor gives an instruction to a man and he goes away on the assumption that the man will carry on. Otherwise he would have to stand over him to see that he did his job and someone would have to stand over the supervisor and so on *ad infinitum*. Thus the "police force" would be bigger than the operative force, which is untenable.

In our cultures—our ways of life—we rely on conscientious people. The transport systems; the public utilities; the wage packets or cheques arriving on time; the postal service; that people will turn up to a meeting when they agree to; and so on. In fact this civilization would collapse unless they did. And so we must establish mutual recognition of relative responsibility at the outset.

Individual Infringement

But not everyone plays the game; some exploit the situation; some individuals infringe.

But it is *individuals* who infringe, and so we must not deprive the group of a facility or attack the group for the misdemeanours of the few. There is a tendency for some people to cite exceptional cases of, say, exploitation of a service, as a weakness or defect in the service and not as a fault of the "infringer", e.g. exploitation of unemployment benefits and redundancy payments.

Individuals Infringe and they Should be Treated as Such

This is not a public problem. We need to isolate the individual from the group and it is useless to attack a person in public. He is on the stage. He will fight you strongly rather than lose face in the eyes of his mates. Hence the importance of a private office, the desk behind a door, where we can treat the individual separately and where we can hope to educate him to accept our standards.

Need to Educate

The first question to ask of the individual in this kind of situation is always "Why?" There may be a good reason for the unacceptable behaviour, if we did but know it. Ask "Why?" because our first principle is mutual recognition of relative responsibility. Get him to talk. Unearth the facts.

This process of educating the person who has infringed can be a slow process, involving many minor disappointments. Some people's standards are very low, and it takes many attempts to lift them, finally, above the horizon of satisfactory conduct. A principle of gradualness applies.

Later in this chapter I propose to develop this area in some detail in discussing counselling and discipline, but for the moment want to establish the fact that the attitudes which people take up are complex structures with three components:

(a) Ideas from suggestion.
(b) Ideas from logical appeals.
(c) Biases and prejudices from the sentiments.

Changing attitudes

It can be seen then that attitudes cannot be changed by logical arguments because this does not deal with all the roots—all the components—and, in particular, it leaves very considerable resistance which has its origin in the sentiments.

If, then, we want to change attitudes, we must bring all the components into the picture.

What methods have we at our disposal for doing this?

The only one I know is to *involve people in decision making—consultation and discussion.*

Consultation and Discussion in Persuasion

Let us look at discussion bearing in mind the outline persuasion chart (Fig. 10a) on p. 78.

In discussion, logical arguments are exchanged across the group, but these are weighted by the prestige of people making them. Thus when the old man says, "In my experience this is so", then *age* weights his argument. When the high-ranking person says, "I think this is a good idea", then *rank* weights the argument. When two or three say, "Don't be so silly, of course he's right", then *number* weights the argument. And when someone throws a book on to the table saying, "I don't know what you are talking about, it's down here in black and white", then the *printed word* clinches the argument.

Thus in discussion, *logical appeals and suggestion* get inextricably mixed. But this is not the important point—the group members arrive at a conclusion and, because the individual members took part in the decision making, the sentiment is right. They are emotionally identified with the solution.

We will never change a person's attitude until he is intellectually and emotionally identified with the proposition.

Informal consultation, involving people in decision making, is the cement of human relations. Consultation is almost as sure a rule about people and attitude change as is the fact that if you put steel outside it will rust.

Forming Favourable Sentiments—The Size of the Problem

Some examples, showing the size of this problem of attitude change, of the resistance of the sentiments, and the application of the principle of participation, may not be out of place at this stage.

During the war some munition factories used to fill 20 mm Hispano shells with explosive and other compositions. These shells were made by Raleigh Cycle, British Mark Grantham, and various Ministry of Supply component factories. They would arrive in big consignments and would be degreased for filling. The unit would fill 10,000, another 10,000, and so on and, finally, be left with a remnant of, say, 560. These went into the stores. The next time it might be 329, and so on. Well, after some months of operation the stores were crowded to the doors with perfectly good remnants which could not be used because there was a rule which said, "Lot numbers and manufacturers cannot be mixed".

Now all these shells were machined to the same specification with agreed tolerances, and we filled in explosives—also to certain specifications and tolerances. It is obvious that rejects would be produced when all the variances went together adversely one way or the other, but for a good deal of the time these variations within the tolerances would compensate each other. And so someone said, "Why can't we fill a mixed lot occasionally and put up with any freak rejects?" Accordingly I was sent an experimental order in which I was to fill a random sample of these remnant shells under controlled conditions and report on what I found.

The Experimental Department completed this order with something like the results we had predicted earlier, and I wrote a report to the Region setting out:

(a) What we set out to do.
(b) What we actually did.
(c) What we found.
(d) What we would recommend.

After about a month I was sent for and it was pretty obvious in the first 5 minutes that I was on the carpet. They did not like the idea of this report, and after a few sharp exchanges the Officer in Charge said: "Let us see what we can recover from this work."

Conference Technique*

His first question was What exactly were we trying to do? (Can I recommend this to you—What exactly is the problem you are trying to solve?)† We agreed on this and so he entered this on a blackboard in the conference room.

"All right—that's what we set out to do; now, what did you do?" This seemed to be acceptable, and so this went on the board.

"What happened next?" and so on.

At the end of 3 hours there was a series of lines of writing on the blackboard. The Officer in Charge read these with suitable links and said: "Well, that's *our* report." Notice *our* report, not Hughes's report.

* American technique where a blackboard is used to record the progress of the discussion *for all to see and check* (as distinct from private recording and personal notes which can be biased and distorted).

† A senior manager once said to a number of young graduates: "I am quite prepared to help any of you young men to solve your problems on two conditions. One is that you have written down on a piece of paper exactly what the problem is, and, secondly, that you have written on another piece of paper what you have done about it already." He has had no problems.

Then he said "Now what did you say?", and he turned to my report and read the summary. The verdict: "Pretty well the same, but different words. We will accept your report."

Now I had sent a logical document setting out the details of the work and this was at first rejected. So much for the logical appeal. But 3 hours later, when the small committee had argued it out for themselves, they reached the same conclusion. They now accepted it. The sentiment was right. My point is that it would take between 5 and 10 minutes to read the report. It took another 2 hours 50 minutes to sell it. This is the size of attitude change. This is the affect of the sentiment.

But why spend time on discussion and consultation—why not just tell people? The answer, of course, is that the time spent at the outset is far less than the time spent later in correcting confusion, dispute, or in countering low morale.

A second example was noticeable in Leicester in 1961. It said in banner headlines 2 feet high—right across the street—"You must save water". I would have preferred "*We* must save water" to ensure co-operation.

A group of mining deputies was visiting a manufacturing firm and the foreman in one department speaking to the visitors said: "I made 1000 of these last week." One of the more thoughtful of the deputies said: "What! You did? You did very well, didn't you."

This shows the importance of avoiding the words "I" and "you" if we are asking for co-operation. The words "we" and "us" are much more appropriate. If you go to your boss and say, "I think this, and I think that, and I think the other", then you cannot really expect him to be interested because you have left him out of it.

Selling an Idea—Harnessing the Sentiments

At one time we used to stick paper washers on to detonators using a dab of shellac and manual location of the washer. There was a considerable number of rejects and a messy shop. Rejects came from excess shellac and faulty location. My senior officer at the time told me to clean up this shop and devise a better process.

There were two problems—excess shellac and bad location. To get rid of the shellac problem we shellaced sheets of paper then stamped washers out of them. This in effect produced shellaced washers. We then put the washers shellaced side uppermost in a holder free enough to fit the detonator. Next we moistened the lugs of the detonator on a methylated spirits pad and inserted it upside-down on to the shellaced surface of the washer in the holder. We put several of these in a tray, put a slight pressure on the top, and left the set to dry. On dismantling, we had perfect location (in the holder) and minimum shellac on the paper.

This arrangement was then developed for a production layout with a reasonable flow of work and with coloured bays and coloured trays to ensure adequate drying time. We were then ready to go, the technical part of the job being completed.

To put the scheme into operation I approached the overlooker on the first shift in the morning, discussed the difficulties of the existing set up with him, and invited him to look at and comment on the arrangements we had made in the new shop. I explained everything to him and asked what he thought of it. He was reasonably impressed, but suggested a slight modification to the layout to meet what he knew would be his labour problem. This did not make any fundamental change in the arrangement, and so this modification was accepted.

We then brought in the operatives and explained the arrangement to them, and in 2 hours the new scheme was working smoothly.

In view of the success of this approach in the morning, we repeated this method for the afternoon shift with a similar result, but as the time neared 7 o'clock in the evening, I decided to go home on the factory transport system to get some food and sleep. Accordingly I said to the overlooker on the afternoon shift, "You tell the overlooker on the night shift exactly what I have told you, and tell him I will come in between 2 and 3 o'clock in the morning to see how he is getting on and to deal with any problems." Then I went home. When I returned early the next morning I found chaos; not only chaos but the overlooker agitating against me and the method—"New-fangled ideas, why can't they leave us alone."

Now at the time I was puzzled. "There can't be anything wrong with the process, it worked perfectly in the morning and afternoon. What is different tonight?" And then I realized.

Here was a supervisor, responsible for the efficient working of a section. I had completely altered his process for him and I had not even taken the trouble to see him about it. I had told him second hand and, what is more, I was coming back to see how well he was doing it. No wonder he was furious.

When I realized this, I went to the man and said "Look, I am sorry I wasn't here to see you at 10 o'clock. I thought it might be better if I came back a little later to see if I could help, when you had had a chance to get used to the scheme."

I apologized. I should have been there however inconvenient this was. And so we started again. I explained the situations to him and listened to what he had to say by way of improvement, and once more the process worked smoothly.

I hope I never make that mistake again. The principle we can extract here is as follows. We must first get the individual to admit there is a problem. (Why should he change if he cannot see a problem?) We need then to suggest a general line of attack on the problem because, as he rightly says, this is our job. But we need now to leave room for additions and suggestions. In fact it might be unwise to tie up all the ends because then he would be faced with a *fait accompli*. There is no room for consultation.

But, you may say, "This takes time". So it does, but this is the time it takes to sell an idea and it represents the time necessary to deal with the sentiment. In my experience it has always taken several times longer to sell an idea than it has to plan a new scheme and complete the necessary equipment.

Consultation is a basic management principle and tool which is ignored at our peril.

Counselling and Discipline

Case History Approach

Persuasion cannot be left without some look at discipline and counselling. I propose first to look at counselling and then at the disciplinary interview and then try to establish that the two are the same.

The technique used in this section will be largely that of the incident approach—the case history.

These cases are included to throw light on abnormal relationship situations and, in particular, develop the ideas summarized in the central area of the persuasion chart (Fig. 10a) on p. 78—logical appeals:

Mutual recognition of relative responsibilities.
Individual infringement.
Need to educate.

The notes in the bottom right-hand corner of the chart are also relevant.

In the early 1950's Norman Rimmer, then the Educational and Training Secretary of the British Institute of Management (B.I.M.) had been active in organizing supervisor courses in the various adult residential centres in the country. He had involved me in several of these and so I was not surprised when one day I received a telephone call from him asking if I would speak to a joint conference of B.A.C.I.E. (British Association for Commercial and Industrial Education), B.I.M., and Roffey Park. The lecture was to be at Roffey Park, near Horsham in Sussex. I knew B.A.C.I.E. and B.I.M. but did not know about Roffey and guessed it was an adult centre like the others. I asked what was the topic and the reply was, "We want you to talk about all the factors involved in the teaching–learning situation and we challenge you to produce a visual aid with all the variables on it."

I was not surprised about this link between management and teaching because in many elements these are essentially the same, but was intrigued by the challenge to produce the visual aid.

The lecture was to be given early on Tuesday morning and I

accepted, assuming that I would travel down on the Monday evening; but owing to unexpected alterations in my own work schedule I found that I must travel overnight, leaving Northampton at 9 p.m. My plan was to drive overnight to within shouting distance of Roffey Park, have a doze in a lay-by, and drive in at about 8 a.m. for a wash, shave, and breakfast.

Everything went well until I reached Horsham at about 2.30 a.m. Here I was faced with alternative routes and so got out my maps to locate myself. Just as I was about to drive away I saw a policeman coming towards me. I knew it was no use driving away because he would stop me and ask me what I was doing there at that time in the morning and so I waited until he came up. He said "What do you want?" I said "I am looking for Roffey Park". He looked at me a little queerly and then said, "You're a bit late aren't you?"

"Well, I started late," said I with a cool attitude. "All right, where's your licence, insurance, etc."

But nothing was wrong. He then came and sat in the passenger seat (why I don't know unless it was to see if I had been drinking) but he found nothing wrong. So then he said: "If you drive along this road (pointing) you will see a big house on the side of the road about 5 miles out. That's Roffey Park". This is what I expected, but I was annoyed because I thought he was suspicious and would ring up Roffey to warn them I was on the way and I did not want anyone to be disturbed. Well, true enough, about 5 miles out there was Roffey Park.

I drove on to the terrace and whilst there was an odd light or two about, decided I would not make myself known until I saw some people moving around. I must have dozed off, because it was light when a nurse came out of the house and up to the car saying, "Aren't you coming in, we've been waiting for you!" I explained who I was and again was treated a little suspiciously and was told I was in the wrong place; I wanted the training centre on the other side of the road. But very helpfully she said: "Have a nap on one of these beds which the doctors use and I will tell them you've arrived when they are moving around."

At about 8 a.m. she came in with a cup of tea, grinning all over her face and said, "It's all right, they are expecting you" (and then the explanation). A policeman rang us up about 2.30 a.m. saying, "One of your old patients is coming back and the rear of his car is full of sheets of asbestos." They had been waiting for quite a long time wondering what I was going to do because I was in a rehabilitation centre for cases whose problem of adjustment had a psychological factor. (The sheets of asbestos were my charts on large sheets of Essex board.)

So much for the kind of expectations we build up around the associates of certain kinds of establishment.

Roffey Park Rehabilitation Centre

That was my introduction to Roffey Park. At the time Roffey Park was run by a Dr. Ling and a well-known psychiatrist Dr. Tredgold. They believed in mental first aid and that management cannot avoid being involved in the early stages of breakdown or in the final rehabilitation of such persons into industry. Tredgold argued that a great many of the cases in Roffey Park at the time need not have been there if experienced, responsible industrialists had known what to do in the early stages. Accordingly, a training centre to help teach the principles of mental first aid was established nearby, and this was the place where I was to lecture.

Both Tredgold and Ling wrote books on their experiences and below are two extracts from Tredgold's *Human Relations in Modern Industry* which I quote to show, first, what Roffey Park was, and, secondly, what was Tredgold's case for mental first aid:

There were already certain centres for physical rehabilitation, and Roffey Park naturally came to pay particular, but by no means exclusive attention to those whose difficulties of adjustment had a psychological factor; though it was, and is, one of its principles that rehabilitation must be a composite process, part physical, part mental, part social—*the third by no means least in importance*. [p. 178.]

But the stimuli of two major wars and of innumerable major road accidents have led to the dissemination of the principles of physical first aid throughout the country, so that there can now be few of us who have escaped a course of lectures on the subject. It has become obvious how much good can come of it. Yet the principles are very simple and consist really of three points only—first, a minimum of specialized knowledge, including the recognition of a few pitfalls to avoid; second, the ability to use one's common sense; third, the development of a simple skill, which can become effective before it is of a high order. Without in any way wishing to deprecate the value of physical first aid, it does not really amount to much more than this. *The principles of mental first aid are the same and can and should be learnt by all.* [p. 139.]

Read also Chapters II and XI; see also p. 31, Complex.

Physical and Physiological Causes of Unusual Behaviour

The object of the following section is to look at some of the situations about which Tredgold was talking and the kinds of situations the manager or supervisor might meet and some of the possible lines of action by way of mental first aid he might take.

I was walking down the corridor of a technical college one day when I saw a fellow progressing in a most extraordinary fashion. I watched the lad for some time, saw that the movements were regular and not those of a person playing the fool and decided that here was a spastic—able to study but not able to do very well with these movements because of brain injury. This is the unusual behaviour—not of someone being a nuisance but having its origin in a physical cause.

Again, a defective thyroid gland in the early years can give rise to the cretin—the idiot dwarf. Stunted body, coarse skin, lank hair, tongue too big for its mouth so that it protrudes and an intellect to match. Some problems, then, have their origin in a physiological cause. William McDougall* has defined temperament (that general quality of behaviour) as due to the effect of glandular secretions in the blood stream, and, in fact, the Spens Report† says this of adolescence:

> The best contemporary opinion now, on the whole, favours a simpler theory. All the apparent modifications of character are regarded as being only the secondary results of the one fundamental change ... the maturing of the sexual glands and organs.

---

* *An Outline of Psychology*, William McDougall, Methuen, 1923, p. 354.
† *Secondary Education* (Spens Report), H.M.S.O., 1938, p. 122.

... And the glandular changes which the maturing involves, are now known to be capable of initiating profound changes in physique, intellectual growth, emotion and temperament.

Psychiatrist and Psychologist

The preceding section suggests that the student of abnormal behaviour needs first a medical training in order to decide whether the behaviour under observation has its origin in a physical or physiological cause, and, if this fails, he must look for a psychological cause.

Thus a psychiatrist, who specializes in abnormal behaviour, needs a training in medicine and also in psychology. The psychologist on the other hand deals with all behaviour of which abnormal behaviour is a part. We would not expect a psychologist to be especially knowledgeable about abnormal behaviour but to have an appreciation of it.

Inferiority Complex

Now let use look at some of the problems Tredgold had in mind. Let us first consider the inferiority complex.

It is quite common for a person to say of another who is humble and retiring, "Oh, he has an inferiority complex". But a person who is humble and retiring has not an inferiority complex—he is merely exhibiting a healthy instinct of self-submission. He recognizes a superior force and is humble in the face of it. An inferiority complex shows itself in the form of exaggerated behaviour, strutting, swaggering, boasting, wearing loud clothes in an attempt by the individual to call attention to himself through his unusual, exaggerated behaviour because he has not been able to call attention to himself through his normal behaviour.

What is the explanation?

Suppose a small stream was trickling near the side of a building and it was suspected that it was undermining the foundations. What could we do? We could, of course, tip one or two loads of earth and rubble into the stream, some distance away, to make a dam. But very soon the water would well up behind the dam and when the pressure was sufficient, burst the dam and surge forward in a flood, possibly to do considerable damage. But, you might say, no engineer would do this; he would reinforce this dam with concrete and make it strong enough to retain a very considerable volume of water. What would happen then? The water would rise behind the dam and overflow and start to trickle into the adjacent premises much to the annoyance of the residents, who would soon be loud in their complaints. But no engineer would do this either; he would know that the water had to go somewhere and might build a dam, but would also provide a culvert down which to channel the water, possibly to drive a paddle wheel, to drive a generator, to light the building whose foundations it was originally threatening. (Perhaps a slight exaggeration, but this is the idea.)

What is the parallel in the human being? If a person is naturally rather active and a little assertive, he can find himself in situations which can obstruct this drive. The individual may stand this for a time until the pressure builds up and there is a violent outburst, sometimes very awkward to control. But if this restraint is so systematic, either deliberately imposed, e.g. a fond parent doing all the thinking for the child in order to protect him from the world—or accidentally imposed by the work setting and policies, then the energy of this powerful assertive drive has to go somewhere, and we find it exhibiting itself in this extravagant exaggerated behaviour which few of us like.

But if we realize that the individual has to achieve recognition in some way, we will make use of these powerful drives in a socially useful way. This is known technically as sublimation.

There are obvious examples of this when we find work of responsibility for a person who is causing trouble on the shop floor. If a person is continually finding fault with the committee—put him on the committee. We see it many times in the home. The younger child is playing on the carpet with a toy belonging to the older child. The older child rushes in and says, "I want my toy!" What does the mother do? She does not take the toy from the younger child immediately, but she says to the youngster, "Here you are, here's your dad's watch", and the exchange is made.

And so we never say, "Stop", we always say, "Do this instead". Provide an alternative activity which is socially acceptable. Thus no psychologist has ever said we should let people do as they like for fear of the development of complexes. He has always recommended, "Do this instead", and hoped that the new activity is socially acceptable.

Extending this idea a little further, some managements have seen that a good recruitment line for foremen is shop stewards, believing (perhaps erroneously) that the energy displayed as a shop steward is better socially used in the work of the foreman.

To resolve the complex we need to recognize the acceptable work of the individual so that he need not engage in extravagant behaviour to call attention to himself.

Industry can help by avoiding conditions of acute and continuous frustration as far as possible and by giving, where convenient, opportunities for satisfactory self-expression in the creative activities of the organization and in consultation.

Claustrophobia

Another class of problem which causes difficulty is illustrated by claustrophobia. I quote a classic example from the late C. W. Valentine's *The New Psychology of the Unconscious* (Christopher, 1932). Before the First World War there was a man who was frightened of confined spaces and felt he must escape from trams and other enclosed spaces. He could not explain this and was very concerned. He found himself in the First World War in dug-outs and trenches, and the stress of the situation was such that he broke down. Luckily for him, he was invalided out of the services and found himself under the care of a Dr. Rivers. (He was fortunate in this respect, but by the time of the Second World War this problem of breakdown under stress of war was more clearly recognized and a large rehabilitation centre existed for this purpose.)

Dr. Rivers set out to find out what was wrong. After some time (ignoring techniques for the moment) he discovered the following. When the man was young he and his sister used to visit a "rag and bone" man to take him odds and ends. One day the door in the passage-way leading to the man's house slammed to and jammed so that they could not open it. At the same time a fierce dog appeared in the entry and "scared the wits" out of these children. The man had forgotten this event, but when he recognized this situation his problem disappeared. He now knew why he was alarmed at confined spaces and he offered to be locked in the deepest bank vault they could find to establish his "cure".

This illustrates the point that some of the unusual behaviour we meet may have its origin in memory traces from unusual or violent experiences earlier, and that the problem does not disappear until these are rationalized and so explained away. It is almost as though these traces represent experiences which are a threat to survival and they will always attract attention until they are "erased from the tape" so to speak by rational explanation—self-discovery.

What kind of techniques, then, are there available for the psychiatrist to unearth—or help the individual to unearth—these causes?

Techniques of the Specialist

The first is obvious. The individual has the facts and he has to communicate them to the psychiatrist; and so the first technique is conversation. Encourage the individual to talk on the assumption that his conversation will in the end return to the area of the trouble, which, like a sore, is continually attracting attention and needs to be salved. A good way to get a person to talk is to repeat the gist of what he has just said. Never lead the conversation, i.e. "It was a poor meal today, wasn't it?"

"A poor meal was it?" (Ball back into his court.)

(We can afford to do a lot more of this in our selection interviews by the way—the panel often talks too much!)

A second technique is a word-association technique, where responses to keywords are recorded and special attention is paid to those words which produce hesitation or even blanks.

A third technique is the ink blot of the Rorschach Test. In early years a blot of ink was made on paper and squashed up. This often produced a symmetrical pattern on the paper when it was opened out. The individual was asked to say what he saw in this. Today printed "standard blots" are available and used, and a "science" has been built up around the kind of responses and kinds of problem case. However, I like to think of the ink blot, like pictures in fires or clouds, as a device to get people to talk.

To this list we can add hypnosis, interpretation of key symbols in dreams, drug treatment, electrical treatment, and, if all these fail, an operation called pre-frontal leucotomy is possible and the personality can be distinctly changed. This was discovered by accident when a workman helping to construct railways in America had the front of his head pierced by an iron spike. This was removed and fortunately he lived. But he was a different man apparently, placid and co-operative and not at all like the powerful assertive individual before the accident. It has been suggested that this kind of operation should be used to modify certain unfortunate (socially) personalities, but as it is not reversible, specialists are naturally very hesitant.

Now when Dr. Tredgold was talking about mental first aid he was obviously not thinking of the responsible industrialist practising all this range of techniques, still less thinking of a man going round with a hammer and chisel to perform an operation called pre-frontal leucotomy on some of his more aggressive employees, supervisors, consultants and managers. In just the same way as in physical first aid no one would expect to set a broken limb (irrespective of how much he knew about it) but would make the person comfortable, put the patient in a position to do no more damage, and get him to a specialist who could set the limb, so Tredgold had limited objectives in mind.

What, then, can the responsible individual do?

The following examples illustrate the possibilties and, in my opinion, represent the kind of thing which Tredgold had in mind in making his appeal.

Examples of Everyday Problems

Some years ago I was involved in running an evening course for the old Ministry of Education/B.I.M. Diploma in Management Studies. The lecture–discussion sessions usually ran from 7 to 9 p.m. in that particular technical college. One night in the middle of the course I was just packing up my equipment at 9 p.m., prior to leaving the building, when a course member came up to the desk and said, "The doctor says I should go one step at a time; what did he mean?" Immediately, I looked at the fellow and could see from his eyes that he was in a state of considerable distress.

What should I do?

Obviously use the first technique—let him talk; and so I said "One step at a time did he say?", and by using this kind of device and an occasional reminder I got a long story. He was very dissatisfied with his present appointment level, believed he could do better, and was applying for jobs—not one stage above, but several stages higher, on the assumption that just after the war he had seen people progress rapidly and, comparing himself with them, did not see why he should not do equally well. He was being rejected—time and again, and this was demoralizing him. Very much under the weather, he had gone to see his doctor who had given the above advice. Now I do not know whether he did not understand what had been said or did not want to accept it, and so he had come to someone else.

I explained to him that after the war it was possible to make rapid advancement if you happened to be available at the time, and this was the reason for some of the unusual successes he had seen, but by the time he was talking to me progress generally had to be one step at a time, and this is what I thought the doctor meant.

The result was considerable relief. The next week he stopped for a few words and again on a third occasion, moving the conversation more and more into topics of course content and the problem seemed to disappear. He stayed the course and was successful.

But there was a problem. This took time—in fact a good half-hour, and even though you yourself may be prepared to give the time, the caretaking staff are usually anxious to clear the building and so you may not only have to give the time but also find the place. Nevertheless, if a person comes to you with a problem of this kind—time or no—space or no—you can do one of two things and not one of three. You either *help*, or you *hinder*. You cannot be neutral. If you decide to help, it will take time. Are you prepared to give the time? Should you be prepared to give the time? Are you a bit of a psychiatrist as well as a psychologist in your capacity as a supervisor/manager/trainer? These are questions which you need to answer.

In my view if you take on people you take on the properties of people; and as you would allow for the properties of materials, tools, and processes, so, too, must you allow for properties of people, and one of the characteristics of people is that they have problems and some very difficult ones which interfere with the work situation.

The second illustration concerns a steward in a building, where I used to work. This steward was an excellent man for the job. He made a point of receiving all members using the establishment. He would have some pleasantries to exchange and would soon find your social interests and after some simple economical exchange he would say, "You're in Room 9 tonight, Sir." He made a point of seeing that everyone knew where he was to go, adding a few words by way of welcome. He was better known than any member of the staff and possibly better remembered.

Now his official job was to supervise the cleaners and generally look after the rooms and their equipment. This meant he had to purchase a few items of equipment, brushes, mops, powders, etc., from time to time and he had also discovered the importance of a cup of tea at a strategic moment. And so he was pleased to make his occasional excursions to purchase the necessary materials and had, in fact, built up a little unit, a job, which he treated with all the care of the professional man he was.

But upstairs in the office was an official. She was not going to have this. No one was going to place orders without her permission, and gradually she was nibbling at his job—destroying his job; his creation in fact.

Well, I got involved from time to time. I would come in late in the evening after an outside lecture and he would be waiting for me.

"Been at me again, Sir." Then I knew I was there for another hour. "Been at you again, have they?", and then out it would tumble. A story which I knew to be true because I knew both sides of the fence. And then, as he talked, with minimum prompting from me, he would reach a stage when he would suggest a line of action for the next day. If I thought it was a good idea I would reinforce his confidence in his decision, but if I could see a real problem, I would say, "Don't you think this will happen—hadn't you better think that one again?" (Notice hadn't *you* better think that one again.)

I never solved any problems for this man. He always solved his own. But he needed someone to talk himself straight on. He knew I would warn him of a dangerous situation. But he solved the problems.

Housewives do this regularly. The husband comes home all worked up, but a few strategic remarks, even grunts, and the husband is steered to rationalize the situation and make better decisions.

If you lose your temper, never make a decision. Postpone a decision and you will find yourself talking yourself straight on someone else, and by the time both sides have done this there is usually a chance of a reasonable compromise.

These are really counselling interviews—not necessarily in an office at all. Encourage the person to talk—he will often solve his own problems.

Notice I have suggested that you be yourself. It is your usual self the person sees as a counsellor. I am suggesting little more than getting a person to talk himself straight.

If he has gone too far, then recommend he sees his, or the factory doctor, and via this route he may find the specialist (the psychiatrist) who can help.

If a person is obviously in trouble and does not make any approaches to you, then it may be necessary to make a few cautious inquiries of his friends. "Jack seems under the weather—is there anything we can do to help?"

Alternatively—wait. It is surprising how a situation will suddenly develop if you are alert to the possibilities.

I believe this is the kind of thing Tredgold had in mind when he recommended mental first aid to reduce the excessive load on rehabilitation centres like Roffey Park. Can we repeat Tredgold's three principles?

1st—A minimum of specialized knowledge, including the recognition of a few pitfalls to avoid.

2nd—The ability to use one's common sense.

3rd—The development of a simple skill which can become effective before it is of a high order.

Disciplinary Interview

So much for the counselling interview; now what of the situation where we believe people to be deliberately difficult—the so-called disciplinary situation.

The word "discipline" has often been associated in people's minds with sanctions and coercion, whereas it might be more reasonable to assume that it is concerned with the mutual acceptance of roles and the balance of rights and responsibilities.

The logical appeal area of the persuasion chart (Fig. 10a, p. 78) focuses attention on three aspects of the problem of discipline:

(a) *Mutual recognition of relative responsibilities.*

The importance of *agreeing* relative responsibilties.

(b) *Individual infringement.*
   The importance of separating the *individual problems* from the *general problems.*
(c) *Need to educate.*
   The possibility of achieving a *better balance* of relationships.

Agreeing Terms of Reference

Many firms subscribe to management by objectives—to the *agreeing of objectives* and to the working out of terms of reference in management development programmes by agreement between senior and subordinate, based on proposals submitted by both parties. But problems arise in:

(a) individuals who do not accept the relative roles, e.g. when one individual is appointed over another who expected the job;
(b) individuals who want considerable freedom to plan their own working methods, i.e. full delegation.

This points to the possibility of a working compromise, an armistice so to speak, and the need only to restrict freedom of action where necessary, as working solutions.

The two case histories which follow illustrate the difficulties which can arise in connection with the acceptance of roles and relative responsibilities.

The Case of the Man who Should have been Appointed

At one time I was appointed as assistant factory development officer in a particular factory and was walking on one of the sections one morning when an office boy came up to me with a scrap of paper torn from an envelope. On the paper it said: "Being as you are taking over my job on Wednesday next, it is about time you came to see something about it!"

This was a considerable surprise for me and so I went to inquire further. The head of the Experimental Department was being sent to London and I had been given his job. The fellow was really angry at this decision as he had a technical man of his own who could have done the job and whom he was sponsoring, and to show his annoyance he scribbled his message on a torn off scrap of paper.

(Suggestion—this is what I think of the decision.)

Now I had to take over a department of some 200 people (technical, supervisory, office, and operative staffs) with something of the order of ninety experimental orders on the books, none of which I knew; and faced with a hostile staff, who, while they did not know me very well, hated the decision and were projecting the fault on me.

This was my introduction to management.

Now my first problem was the technical man who was expecting (or hoping for) the job. What should I do to ensure his co-operation? (This is really discipline in its widest not "sanction wielding" sense.) My guess was that he would resent any restriction from me, and so I did my best to see that undue restrictions should not arise. I knew he liked to make regular trips to the Design Department to discuss new developments. I encouraged this. I knew he liked designing tools, and so I encouraged that and I went further in seeing that he had access to particular kinds of experimental work which he tended to prefer. In other words I went to great lengths to see his difficulty and ease the acceptance of the situation.

But he did nøt respond. Maybe my efforts only irritated him the more, and the consequence was considerable resentment and antagonism. Maybe he had to have someone to fight. At the end of a month I decided that I had failed to educate him to accept the situation. He had not responded to reasonable approaches. I was now reaching for my sanctions.

On the Saturday morning of that week I stopped him as he was about to go off the section and said to him: "Look, I have been falling over backwards in the last month to see your point of view about this appointment. I did not make the appointment, neither did you, but it's going to work. You have deliberately been awkward, but from now on it's going to stop and if it doesn't one of us is going and it won't be me."

I was back on my last weapon after an extended attempt to educate.

Now the fellow was a very able man and intelligent enough to see the position. He stopped. We had an armistice for 3 years. No more than an armistice. When I was away he would always show he could do better. He never recognized I was the man for the job, but we worked together. When I left I recommended him for my job and he nearly fell over backwards. Nothing was too much trouble. The problem had disappeared.

What I am trying to illustrate here is that there are some disciplinary situations which you will never solve, but you can sometimes get a useful working compromise, an armistice, so to speak, which enables work to go on.

Importance of Terms of Reference and Full Delegation

Again, at one time, I had a progress man. He was extraordinarily good. He could get you anything which was in the country, but you never had to ask him how he did it. I could say to him: "There are five of these in X. We want three of these by Thursday night." "O.K.", he would say, "leave it to me", and off he would go and almost invariably the material would be there. But you had not to ask him, "Where were you on Wednesday?" He would not tell you. His attitude was: "Tell me the job—leave it to me—delegate fully and don't interfere."

Now it is relatively easy to employ a man like this, but unfortunately for me I had to report to London every Friday on the state of the projects and so I needed him there as he was progressing my experimental components for me. And so it was necessary (perhaps reluctantly), to agree on some detailed terms of reference.

I went to the head of Production Progress and: said "How do you think Experimental Progress relates to you? Have you any functional relationship?" And he told me what he thought the position was. Then I went to the head of the factory stores, from whom we got basic components, and said, "When this man contacts you for materials, what arrangements do you want to operate?"

I was now armed with evidence as to how this progress man related to the factory; the rest was at my disposal in the Experimental Department. Accordingly I sent for him and said: "Let us agree on your terms of reference. What do you expect me to do for you and what can I expect you to do for me?" In effect I tried to establish "mutual recognition of relative responsibility".

After some time we reached agreement. This was typed out. He had a copy, I had a copy, and I got him to sign them both. Today I would not do this because I believe that if I ask a person to sign a document of this kind it is really saying I distrust him and expect him to manoeuvre. It is good enough to have agreed to the paper. It is not necessary to sign statements about agreed objectives, when we practise management by objectives.

I put my copy on the wall behind me. Some weeks later he came into my office in a state of protest. Such and such a thing was not his job and and he was complaining. My reaction was to reach for the terms of reference and show clearly that he had agreed it was his job. But my further reaction was to say: "Look, don't you tell me you are not going to do your job, because you agreed it was your job—but if, on the other hand, you are saying you know a better method of doing the job then I am quite prepared to discuss it. I don't want any more dead wood than you do."

The situation was settled and it shows how important it is to establish, *right from the outset*, mutual recognition of relative responsibilities, and the act of doing this is the first guarantee of reasonable relationships, i.e. good discipline in the establishment.

This applies to any establishment and any teaching situation as well. Watch your early contacts. Establish good induction procedures.

This man was excellent at his job.

Establishing Safety as an Attitude

The explosives industry's attack on safety illustrates the three elements in logical appeals mentioned earlier on pp. 102, 103:

Mutual recognition of relative responsibilities.
Individual infringement.
Need to educate.

Production groups on explosives-filling factories are very extensive because of the need to separate buildings to minimize explosion risks, but considerable care is exercised about appropriate clothing, procedures, and contraband articles.

The individual will enter a group via a "shift house" or changing room, but before he does so he will pass what is called a contraband hut and must follow a recognized procedure.

Above the contraband hut is a large notice listing articles which must not be taken on to a filling section. These include matches, cigarettes, pipes, tobacco, lighters, hair grips, rings (unless covered), silk underwear, and the like.

As the individual passes the contraband hut, he will say to the man inside, "All clear!" This means I have none of the things listed, on my person. If he has, he hands them to the man to be kept until he comes off the group—"All clear".

He will then proceed to the shift house where he will meet an attendant. He will say again, "All clear", but the attendant need not believe him and can make a token search (as a double security check). If he finds something he will remind the man of his obligations—otherwise he will proceed.

After changing into suitable clothes the individual will step over a low barrier which says "Clean" on one side and "Dirty" on the other and is now in a filling section. It is common to hear him say again, "All clear".

This procedure is aimed at stressing the importance of the regulations—establishing mutual recognition of relative responsibilities.

Now the Chief Inspector for Safety agreed that this would be the prime attack, to be proceeded with every time a person entered a group, but accepting that a number of infringements would occur, especially with "learners" in situations like war emergencies.

There will be the person who says "All clear", forgetting a box of matches he does not normally carry—accidental infringement.

There will be the person who says "All clear" because the person in front of him says "All clear". It is a kind of code word to get you into the group—he doesn't know what it means—a case of bad reception.

There will be the person who says "All clear" knowing full well he has a match and a cigarette about his person and he intends to have a smoke in an air-raid shelter whether you like it, or not.

All these have to be found.

Accordingly, the Chief Inspector for Safety sent danger building visitors round the filling sections to find such offenders and these visitors came up to the office with what they found.

I have been faced with sets of hair grips and the like and left with small bits of paper on which the case was recorded in outline and a space (headed "Action taken") left for completion. In effect I was being told—these are the individuals who have infringed, what do you propose to do about educating these people to accept the safety regulations. You are responsible for safety in your section.

These are perfect examples of what people would call bad discipline—and I am being asked, "What do you propose to do?"

My first reaction could easily be look for some sanction—some big stick.

What about sacking one or two as examples—strong-arm stuff. But it was not possible to sack people during the war except in exceptional circumstances of gross infringement—and so that weapon had gone.

What about 3 days' suspension without pay. That's the answer! But one of my assistant foremen said to me: "These people work long day shifts, the only time they have to spend any money is Saturday afternoon. Some of these girls will be only too pleased to have 3 days off with no pay in order to spend some of the money they have saved. They will come loaded with hair grips, attracting attention, to get time off."

And so the second sanction had gone.

We now had to try to educate without sanctions, i.e. by reason.

I would send for the operators and this time sit them on the other side of the desk to enhance my stature. "Now you see these hair grips? You said 'All clear'. We don't think you would do this if you knew the risk you are taking by wearing them. A hair grip can drop out into a mixture which is being mixed, or pressed, and you can cause a nasty explosion. You can hit T.N.T. with a hammer and it won't go off, but if you give it the right sort of crack, it will blow your hand off. Now we don't think you should take the risk of injuring other people. The prettier you look the better we like it, but you will have to find another way of holding up your hair because hair grips are dangerous."

This kind of argument worked well, but we had great difficulty over silk underwear. Now the problem of silk underwear is the danger of generating static electricity by friction.

We could have had the operators searched as they came through the shift house and could have sent home all those wearing silk underwear. If we had done so, we would have lost the labour force, and we wanted ammunition urgently. So here was a situation where it would have taken too long to educate the person to behave safely and so we had to turn to devices to protect the person against himself.

Principle of Guards and Protective Devices

The door knobs were metal, connected by a thick copper strip to a flexible metal hinge and hence to a copper strip which was earthed. The person earthed himself. Machines and other devices were earthed as far as possible.

This is the principle of guards. If we cannot educate a person to behave safely, we will have to erect guards to protect him against himself. But the more we erect guards the more the person will rely on them and stop thinking.

This is the great dilemma of safety. And so we need to work at both attitude and guards—not just guards.

This attack on safety was so successful in explosives filling that in 3½ years I had only one serious accident in my shops. It seems to me to be a tribute to the three principles of logical appeals in persuasion.

Mutual recognition.
Individual infringement.
Need to educate.

It is important here to remember that our case for persuasion was not really satisfied with logical appeals and insisted on participation in decision making in order to help develop favourable sentiments (in addition to the prestige elements of suggestion). For this reason a great many posters employed in safety work are of little use because these do not involve the observer. Posters need to ask a question—set a problem, e.g. "Which cat is the grandmother?", and straight away you are wondering; you are involved.

Additional Note on Safety and Attitude

A study of the accidents in the steel industry (1967) revealed that 68 per cent of the accidents leading to injury were due to falls; striking against objects; handling operations; falling objects, i.e. the big four. These are the kinds of accident which can happen anywhere. They cannot be the concern of *engineering*, i.e. guards, remote control and the like, or of *enforcement*, but must be the field for *education*, and we can help by trying to ensure safe habits, as described earlier, or by developing safe attitudes to work.

In helping to develop such attitudes our original case was for suggestion, logical appeals, and sentiments as key areas for concern.

Briefly, *suggestion* will depend on the selling effects of a number of prestige elements like age, rank, stature, number, printed word. We can see these best exhibited in the pop stars, sports idols, and the like, and so the practical conclusion is *set an example* because you might be someone's idea of a star—the experienced man, the boss, the man with the big car, the exclusive office.

Logical appeals demand that we agree at the outset on objectives and of course this stresses the importance of the early contacts with people.

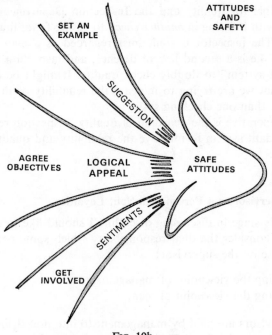

FIG. 10b.

Sentiments call for actual involvement in the decision making and hence the recommendation *get involved* in suggestion schemes, poster designs, and methods of working.

These three points are shown diagrammatically (Fig. 10b) using the early persuasion chart (Fig. 10a) as a model.

The education attack on safety stresses, therefore, the importance of reception, induction, and informal consultation, in aiming at appropriate habits and attitudes.

Quality as an Attitude

In just the same way that safety is very much a question of attitude of mind, so is quality. There is a tendency for the members of the Inspection Department to be regarded as the people who are responsible for quality. It is obvious that the operative is responsible for quality and the Inspection Department is concerned with building in *another check* to ensure fewer faulty parts issued. The inspector is sometimes regarded as a man to beat. Actually he is a second line of defence, and inspection is a "redundant system" to doubly check quality. It might be better to think that we are trying to increase the reliability of the system by more than one checking system.

The operative is the guardian of quality. Inspection represents a redundant system to improve the reliability and quality of the product.

The Supervisor as a Person with Split Loyalties

At this stage in discussing discipline I should like to digress a little to consider the dual responsibility which some people like to impose on the supervisor:

> Seeing the viewpoint of management.
> Seeing the viewpoint of men.

Supervisors are paid by management to interpret their policies on the shop/office floor. Their loyalties are, therefore, to management. They are paid to educate on behalf of management.

Now it is easy to see that when I believe in a regulation I can find arguments to support it and can readily educate on behalf of management, but what happens when I am asked to administer a rule I do not myself believe in—that I think is not appropriate? The following is a case in point.

The principal of an emergency training college said to the assembled staff and students (experienced men and women) one hot summer day, "No man in this college shall wear an open-necked shirt." No reasons were given, no attempt at explanation, either to students or staff—just the plain statement.

On splitting up into small working groups, one tutor reminded two students with open-necked shirts of what the principal had said, saying, "Put a tie on tomorrow, will you." The next day one of the students had complied, but the other had not. The tutor remonstrated with the man, only to be asked: "Why should I wear a tie? I rarely wear a tie." Now the tutor did not know—the principal had given no reason and, what is more, he thought the rule was unreasonable as well. But he stuck to his loyalty to the management team and rationalized by saying: "I suppose the idea is that when you get a job in a school or college, you will have to wear a tie and it is on occasions like this when you might be tempted not to. This is a good time to get used to it."

But the student was not satisfied and wanted to push the matter further. The tutor was now in a difficult position because he sympathized with the student's point of view, but knew he had to educate on behalf of the principal and so he said: "Look, if you feel all that strongly about the matter, why don't you drop in to see the principal to discuss it with him. No doubt he has a very good reason, which he will be only too pleased to discuss with you."

He referred the student to the person above him who was in a better position to educate than he was himself.

Some people regard this as "passing the buck". But you "pass the buck" when you are in full possession of the facts and dislike using them. If you are not in full possession of the facts you are obliged, in fact it is your duty, to refer the person to someone above you who is in a better position to educate than you are.

But the tutor did not stop there. Behind the scenes he saw the principal to report the difficulties (feedback) and ask for information. That is, he represented the interests of the student to management, whilst still staying loyal to management, in an attempt to educate on their behalf.

There is no need for any supervisor to feel split loyalties. He represents management when he educates on their behalf. He can represent the interests of the labour force (students here), by reporting back to management about decisions which are out of touch with reality on the shop floor. Only by such means will improvement be achieved.

Feedback up the chain is essential if the supervisor wants to represent the interests of the people he supervises and still educate on behalf of management.

Of course, if you differ with management on major principles and are always in conflict with management, you should begin to wonder if this is your job—if you can accept payment for interpreting management's policies on the shop floor.

Outside Factors affecting Relationships

Not all problem situations are of your causing. The following example illustrates how outside factors can produce difficult relationships elsewhere.

At one time, in order to earn holiday money, I taught P.T. to some young workers. We had some good sessions and the establishment had a good reputation for this kind of work. One night I was getting the class to do some warming-up exercises before heavy agility exercises, when one youth unexpectedly started to fool around and would not do as he was told.

I remonstrated with the lad mildly at first, but as he still continued to be awkward, gradually increased the pressure until, having failed to educate, I told him to get upstairs and get dressed —my last resort.

He refused to go. I now desperately needed time to think what next to do, when suddenly I remembered the evening school superintendent. I turned to one of the other lads and said, "Fetch the superintendent."

The superintendent duly appeared and asked the trouble. I explained that the lad was refusing to follow my instructions and therefore I could not accept responsibility for him on heavy agility exercises, to which we were about to proceed. I said, "I have told him to get dressed and he refuses to go". And then I made a fatal mistake. I said, "If he doesn't go in the next 2 minutes, I propose to throw him out". This was a foolish statement.

The superintendent said, "You have heard what he said, you had better go". And peculiarly enough, much to my amazement, the lad started to go. I was surprised, but relieved, but when the lad got about 10 yards away, he turned round and called me everything under the sun. My reaction at first was, "Why bother, you have got what you wanted". But suddenly I decided, "Why should I stand this?", and in a flash of temper went after him, picked him up, kicked open the dressing-room door and flung him in. He hit the floor with a resounding thud and I was very satisfied. I slammed the door and went to join the group.

But I paid for it. After the lesson we went upstairs to the dressing-room and he had wrecked the room. There was ink all over the walls, furniture upside down; a real shambles.

Of course we got rid of him, but you might well ask, "Why of course?" Some weeks later I met him in the street and he said, "Can I come back?" I said: "Of course you can come back provided you do as you are told. I have nothing against you but I cannot accept responsibility for students on apparatus unless they do as they are told." Then the story came out. There had been a first-class row at home that night and he had come out gunning for someone. I happened to be the first person he could get at. Some disciplinary problems are not of your making. Personal and domestic issues can interfere with normal relationships.

Counselling and Disciplinary Interview—The Same?

This last point leads naturally to the final section of this chapter—the link between counselling and discipline.

Some time ago a controller in one of the public utilities told this story. A senior official made a decision which closed down a newly commissioned power station. Now this, of course, was a tragedy. The controller said it was his job to deal with the official, but decided that it was no use "tearing a strip off" the man. This would do nothing except temper his annoyance. He said, "He knew what he had done—we all knew what he had done. The problem was *why* had it happened and what could be done to prevent a recurrence." (Note this emphasis—It is no use looking for someone to blame. In my opinion too many people are looking for someone to blame, to no purpose. Look for the *cause*.)

No one deliberately makes a mistake—unless they are bloody-minded, and then there is something radically wrong with the set-up.

Find out What and Why

Accordingly he sent for the man and, using the counselling interview technique, got him to talk to find out the cause.

He discovered that this man and his wife used to live in a town where they had plenty of social contacts. When he went to work he was meeting people and his wife had plenty of friends. They had moved to this new rural area where, when he went to work, he had plenty of colleagues but his wife knew no one. She was isolated and had few social contacts. She was complaining about this isolation and in his preoccupation with this domestic issue he had made a faulty decision, which had closed down a power station.

The authority reacted by finding some social contacts for the man's wife. They had isolated the problem and solved it appropriately.

The whole point here is that the so-called disciplinary situation had become a counselling situation. Is the disciplinary interview really a counselling interview and are sanctions really of doubtful value?

Why do we not try to find out *what is wrong* instead of *someone to blame?*

Changing Emphasis in Relationships

In discussing disciplinary problems it is still possible today to hear management talk of punishing people, and I have heard a trade union official talking to shift managers in terms of "showing mercy" to labour.

This is the language of an earlier generation when it was possible to dispense jobs in the form of bounty and unemployment was a permanent feature of industrial relations and an ever-present threat. It is foreign, however, to a state of society where, since 1945, we have been asking labour to co-operate with management in a joint effort to produce.

As we move more to staff relationship with all labour, so relationships become more those of co-operation between responsible and professional people. The fact that the words "productivity agreement" are in the vocabulary of industrial relations suggests responsible association between management and men. The Donovan Commission recommendation* on the sanction of dismissal, further points the importance of mutual recognition of relative responsibilities as the real basis for association. American writings† on management without a senior–subordinate relationship, current technical supervisory practices in project groups, where we respect the expertise of colleagues, and the growth of the practice of management by objectives (agreeing objectives), all reinforce this concept of responsible relationships.

Reality, then, suggests a meaning for discipline which implies mutual recognition rather than the wielding of sanctions and an implication of a counselling and problem solving approach to relationship questions.

Industrial Relations and Human Relations

The reader might be surprised that this particular area of the book has not referred to the institutionalized methods of regu-

* *Royal Commission on Trade Unions and Employers' Associations 1965–68*, London, H.M.S.O., ch IX, §§ 545, 565.

† J. W. Forrester, A new corporate design, *Industrial Management Review*, **7** (1) (1965).

lating relationships between management and labour, i.e. our systems of industrial relations. We have been concerned rather with the methods whereby co-operative action can be achieved in any setting (including round the negotiating table), accepting that, in the end, we may have to have recourse to a formalized, institutionalized set of procedures to resolve the impasse—accepting also that the existence of this system of industrial relations will affect our human relationship discussions and manœuvres.

The recent discussions on legislative action* represent, of course, the final appeal before chaos. Whilst obviously I do not subscribe completely to the statement that industrial relations starts where human relations finishes, there is still something in the idea that the progression is human relations, industrial relations, legislation.

In this chapter we have made a case for participation in decision making as a powerful device in achieving attitude change. In the appendix a number of practical techniques for promoting discussion and ensuring involvement are described.

* *In Place of Strife*, Cmnd. 3888, H.M.S.O., 1969.

CHAPTER 5

Communication

More than Public Speaking and Report Writing

Many course programmes for management and supervisory groups include a section on communication and almost invariably this covers public speaking and report writing. This obviously implies that oral and written communications are important in industrial communication situations, but one wonders if this is all. In some management courses recently I have been asked to speak to a group on communication over a double session and have agreed to let the second half go wherever the discussion took us. It has almost invariably finished up on human relations topics. Perhaps good communications and good human relations are synonymous.

Some years ago the Physical Society ran a symposium on communication at Bedford College. I was amazed at the range of communication problems represented; noise on telephone systems, semantics, phonetics, the communication problems of cheese testing, and the like. Again, the Communication Research Centre of the University College London produced a book* and this particular volume (which was the first of three) had a series of chapters all dealing with a different class of communication problem. And so I believe my doubt was sustained and that communication should be more than public speaking and report writing in management courses.

In the notes which follow I want to look at communication as

---

* *Studies in Communication, Communication Research Centre*, U. College, London, Secker & Warburg, 1955.

119

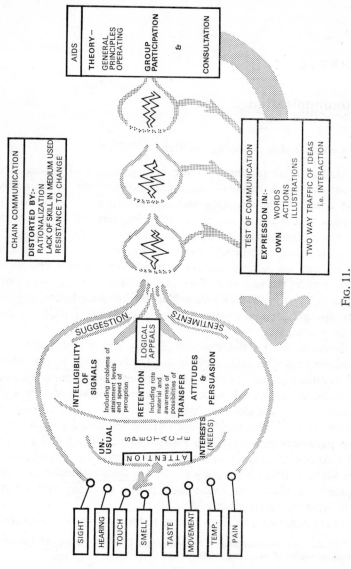

Fig. 11.

fundamentally as my present experience will allow me, dealing with classes of problems and possible industrial/educational implications. The diagram (Fig. 11) has been exploded a little to illustrate the points, but in essence it is a communication loop.

Problem I—Multi-channel Input

The essence of the first problem is that some information is available in the world outside which has to be made available to the central nervous system or, crudely, some information to be got into someone's head. Accordingly we have to ask oursleves: What channels are available to achieve this end?, and the answers will be obtained by asking ourselves the further question: How are we aware of the outside world?

We can see things; we can hear things; and we can smell things occasionally; we can feel things; we can taste things. In short, the five senses.

But some of these are better than others for specific purposes. For example, I don't *tell* people what silk *feels* like. I arrange a series of fabrics—ask the individual to feel them and then point out the one which is silk. When I go to the tailor he feels my coat and says, "This isn't a bad piece of cloth." I feel it with hima nd might give the impression I know, but I do not know because I do not do it often enough. Again, during the war in A.R.P. (air-raid precaution) lectures, we said that the gas phosgene smells like musty hay. But no one ever attempted to tell people what musty hay smelt like, they passed round a bottle with material simulating the smell and said, "It smells like this".

The principal of a technical college was once asked how he trained his apprentices. He said, "Do you know, I don't know. I'd better find out." So he said to an instructor, "How do you train the apprentices in the basic training workshop?" The man said, "Oh, we give them this to do, and that, and the other." But the principal said, "I don't mean that. How do you teach them what kind of pressure to put on a tool before they damage it?" The instructor said, "We don't, they find out for themselves".

Notice that you cannot teach a person how to file. You can put him into a position to approach the work well; tell him how to hold the file and comment on the filings and the finish. But you cannot tell him what it feels like when the tool is cutting well.

It is obvious then that in industrial training in particular, senses other than sight and hearing are going to be very important and for this reason time spent giving people actual experience of the properties of materials, rather than talking about them only, is well spent and in fact essential. Workshop practice and laboratory experience are therefore vital, despite their time-consuming nature.

There are many arguments for limiting training experiences, but we must wonder whether it is possible to telescope some experiences.

Again, in negotiating situations it is a good principle to inspect the place of dispute before making a decision.

Furthermore, recruitment literature can only convey some information about the work situation; a tour of the premises is necessary to supplement the information in the career booklet.

In another context a Scandinavian professor of physics speaking at the opening of Newcastle University said that there are two problems which are vital today. Firstly, how to communicate to other people ideas about new concepts in physics for which the language of classical physics is inadequate (not a question of literacy), and, secondly, the question of statistics.

So far we have said that some of the five senses are more important (always) than others in communicating certain information, but it should also be remembered that some people prefer others as well.

At one time my sister-in-law was due to come for a visit to a new house and my wife was writing to her about the visit. I said, "Tell K— I will draw him a sketch map to show him how to get here". My wife said, "That's all right, my sister can read. I've told her! Get away with your pictures, we are literate in our family!" On the other hand, some engineers cannot talk without scribbling some little diagram on the paper or on a table top or on a wall to illustrate what they mean.

I once damaged my gear box and the mechanic in the garage said, "Oh, you've broken a tooth on the main cluster, I think". But by looking at my face (I did not say a word) he realized I was not following and so he picked up a screwdriver and carved a picture on the bench and then pointing he said, "It's gone wrong here", and immediately he realized I knew.

Thus some sense channels are more effective than others and some are preferred by others. We must not forget we are communicating with others—not with ourselves.

But there are more than five channels. Suppose you stop a person in the street and ask for a direction; if the person is wise he will face the same way as you and he can say, "Oh, you go straight up here and go round the roundabout to the left", indicating by the movement of his arm a turn to the right. In these circumstances, I guess that most people would think that the person had confused his words left and right, but would have no hesitation in accepting the movement as a clear indication of what was intended—a turn to the right.

Again: Which way do you tighten a woodscrew? (corkscrew, if you prefer)—clockwise. Notice, movement first, description after.

It is surprising how delicately these input channels are balanced as any one will know who has had his "frame-hold" fail when information from the semicircular canals and the eustachian tube has been distorted by catarrh.

To the list of channels we can add temperature—we can appreciate differences in temperature, not actual temperature.

Finally, we can appreciate information via the sense of pain.

Thus there are, at least, something like eight different channels which are available to us for information purposes and some of these are more effective than others. J. Arthur Thomson suggests the number is nearer twenty than five senses.*

* J. Arthur Thomson, *Biology for Everyman*, Dent, 1934, p. 1313.

Competing Channels

But if there are many channels, why not feed information into them all simultaneously? (In fact, of course, this is what is happening.) But the problem is: Can the central nervous system pay attention to several channels simultaneously? Experiments have thrown doubt on this possibility but this need not prove a big obstacle because, as a cinema film shows, we need only pay attention to a regular flow of "stills" (i.e. not something which is continuous) and assume that the situation has been progressing uniformly in the gaps. Thus we can scan the input rapidly and only return at regular intervals to check progress (as the performer does when he spins a whole set of plates in a juggling act).

A biologist* lecturing in one of our management courses said that if you scratch the back of the neck of a dog in certain circumstances it will make a scratching movement. If you press the pad of the foot it will stiffen the leg. What happens if you scratch the neck and press the pad at the same time? The answer is the dog stiffens its leg. This means, of course, that it prefers to run away (to engage in the luxury of scratching another day).

Thus the reflex system here does not respond to two stimuli simultaneously, but selects the one which is best suited to survival.

Problem II—Attention

The second class of problem in communication then is—*How do you get attention to a given set of signals*? That is, how do we get the scanning to stop where the selected information is being fed; out of all the competing stimuli—noise, temperature, pressure of seat, glare from lights, digestion processes—how can I get a person to attend to my communication?

The Unusual

The first answer is do something unusual. Biologically we attend to the unusual in our environment because it is the unusual

* Dr. Bish, Head of Biology Department, Leicester Regional College of Technology.

element in our environment which represents a threat to our survival. "We notice differences", says Bartlett, "and have to be taught to notice similarities."*

Thus fluorescent paint made quite an impact on posters on hoardings; but when everyone used fluorescent paint we no longer noticed. If a light flashes we will notice it, but if it flashes continuously we won't even know it's there. Thus we can overdo displays and leave notices up too long. They become the usual and the effect of the unusual has gone.

A civil engineer said recently that the members of his staff were coming to work on time but were failing to clock-on. And so he put up a notice (which was nicely phrased), saying, "Have you clocked?" This had quite an impact, yielding a good response. After a time the position deteriorated to the old work habits. He was puzzled until he realized that the notice had become part of the background and no longer made an impact as an unusual element.

This means that permanent notices need to be moved, resited or refurbished from time to time, if they are still to have an impact as an unusual element in the environment.

The unusual then is one way of getting attention, but, by definition, can only be used unusually.

The Spectacle

The second method of getting attention is via the spectacle. If you climb a mountain and the clouds blow away, you may find yourself looking at a view you have never seen before and you find yourself just looking at it. You do not wish to alter it or modify it—a perfect communication. Now every artist tries to do this. He tries to contrive a situation where you have forgotten everything else and are just hanging on that next note, the next word, the next movement. But they achieve this rarely because it de-

* Emeritus Professor Sir Frederick Bartlett, *The Mind at Work and Play*, Allen & Unwin, p. 118,

pends on the concurrence of a considerable number of variables, not all under their control. In 30 years of lecturing I have achieved this about three times—people hanging on every word and doing just what was wanted. But this depended very much on a number of preceding and current events. Thus we cannot rely on, but only hope for, the spectacle.

What, then, is the third method?

Basic Needs

If I break my leg I will listen to anyone who knows something about first aid because it is important to me to do something about the situation. If a housewife has just scalded the baby's leg she will find the health visitor a very welcome visitor. But, of course, the problem of the health visitor is to try to get mothers interested in the hazard of scalding babies' legs when they have not done so.

What, then, is the key?

People will pay attention to those things which affect their basic needs and I have to predict what these are likely to be at the time I wish to make my communication.

The problem of the siting of notice boards illustrates this. If people are queuing up for some particular purpose on one side of a serving hatch (or bob hole) they may read your notice when they are moving slowly with nothing particular to do. But if you move the notice to the other side of the hatch, they are away. Their present need satisfied—no time to stay. You can move a notice by a yard and it will not be read.

Similarly, notices placed near clocking stations are ignoring the fact that people passing through the clocking stations are either in a great hurry to get in or, alternatively, to get out, and they are not likely to stay to read. Detailed notices, then, need to be placed where people are moving slowly and with nothing particularly urgent to do.

The earlier work in this text on reception procedures has also focused attention on the importance of siting notices to meet the needs of new entrants for useful information and directions. A great deal of attention has been paid in recent years to this problem, and this is well instanced in the new road developments.

For over 6 years I travelled between the Midlands and the North-East using the Great North Road (A1). For most of this time the A1 was in a state of reconstruction and yet I was never embarrassed at any time. I was switched from track to track in the various diversions, but never hit a barrier or was seriously obstructed, even on the blackest night and in the poorest visibility; and the reason was that notices were put up well in advance, allowing for reasonable speeds, gradually pushing people over to the required track. This suggests very considerable attention to communications which has characterized some contractors and the general design of communications on the motorways. On the other hand, one can think of other major alterations when it was difficult to find one's way even in the daylight.

Again, it is interesting to see the use of lower-case printing for ease in reading and the use of block capitals for emphasis.

Yet despite all this attention to communication on the motorways I still find it difficult to write down exactly what it says at the entrance to the motorways. I realize, in fact, that I have paid attention only to those things which affect my basic requirements and have only a vague idea of the rest of the instructions.

Continuing this idea of basic needs, it is easy to see how communications placed inside or alongside a pay envelope will get scant attention when the individual is really concerned with what money is in the envelope.

Again, unfortunate wording can produce bad reactions, even resistance, as in the following line:

Members of the staff *will* . . . .

instead of

Will members of the staff. . . .

Problem III—Intelligibility of Signals

If we supppose that we can get attention, what then is the next class of problem? It is, of course, whether the signals which are being used are intelligible to the observer.

I was travelling south from Newcastle early one morning and I picked up two men. In the course of conversation it turned out that they were going to London to try to find a job. One of them said to me, "What is unemployment like in Newcastle at the present time?" I replied, "It's about 5 per cent." He said, "Oh, yes", seemingly satisfied, but the other fellow said to him, "What did he say?", and then I listened, very intently, to a detailed explanation as to what I meant by 5 per cent. I had thought carelessly (I should have known better) that everyone knew what I meant by 5 per cent and this was a real reminder to me about the intelligibility of signals.

The use of letters by way of abbreviation can lead to confusion through unintelligibility and ambiguity. Industrial training staffs will readily understand the signals T.W.I.—J.I., but the beginner will not know that this refers to a training programme called Training Within Industry—Job Instruction. But even the expert will not know in the aerospace industry whether the B.A.C. means British Aircraft Corporation or Bristol Aeroplane Company.

We need to ensure that our abbreviations are likely to be intelligible.

Again, if we look at notices of the typewritten or detailed type, we will notice that the language is often the language of middle management. This is very satisfactory if we are communicating with middle management, but not satisfactory if we are communicating to people with less experience of the written medium.

Signals lose their intelligibility if their size is not adjusted to the speed at which people are moving. And there is quite a deal of evidence that the printing is too small in some road advertising campaigns, especially those of a local nature.

It is interesting to test whether it is possible to read the notices at the entrance to the motorways at the speed which the approach roads permit.

Colour is useful to help make a complicated diagram intelligible. It helps to separate complex black-and-white material into areas and then we look for details within the area. I made the mistake once of producing photostat copies of a map, used for research purposes, on which the details had been entered in colour. The original was very clear, but all the detail disappeared and was confused in the black-and-white version. Photographs are better in this respect because they depend on reflected light and come out in shades of grey. Even here colour can help.

Problem IV—Retention, Memory, Recognition, and Recall

When we are sure that the signals put up are intelligible, the next class of problem is: Will they be retained? It is important that they be retained, unless the initial experience was intended by way of entertainment. Here we have two problems:

(a) Memory for rote (illogical) material.
(b) Transfer of experience.

Rote Material

People's names, dates, part numbers (the first part of a number can be a code, but the last part is a random number) and such material, i.e. rote material, sometimes needs to be memorized. Now there is usually nothing about a person to suggest his name is Mr. Smith. Thus if I want to remember that X is Mr. Smith, there is no way out of this except that of continually repeating Mr. Smith when X appears. Thus I should say, "Good morning, Mr. Smith", and not, "Good morning", or in courses, for example, use name cards so that by continually associating X with Mr. Smith, I have no difficulty later in trying to recall the name of X when I am assembling a team to work on a given project, or wish to introduce Mr. Smith to a visitor.

With rote material, then, there appears to be nothing for it except hard work in repetition, and we need to engineer situations to provide such repetition.

In short course work, which is common these days, lectures are often supplemented by hand-out material. This means that course members can just listen instead of taking notes. Many course members prefer to listen because the act of note-making gets in the way, but, on the other hand, repetitions are eliminated by such techniques in contrast to other teaching situations where many repetitions are engineered—oral and written—with repetitions performed by teacher and by student in talking, discussing, writing on blackboard, and recording in note form.

There is, of course, the idea of mnemonics as aids to recall, which people invent when they are very anxious to retain certain material, e.g. Eat Good Bread Dear Father for E, G, B, D, F—the notes on the lines of a music stave treble clef.

Recall and Recognition

At this stage it might be worth while to digress a little and look at the difference between recall and recognition in connection with memory. The difference has considerable implications in industry and education.

If I read a textbook when I am revising for an examination, I can recognize the material I see on the page and think I am familiar enough with it to be able to reproduce it.

But when I am asked to reproduce it on the examination paper (as we are sometimes required to do for factual material), I have to recall it from everything else I have experienced and, of course, this is more difficult. Thus recognition is easier than recall, but it is important to remember that in examinations we are usually asked to recall something and not to recognize it as true. We should therefore in our revision try ourselves out on a scrap of paper, without looking at the book, in order to check that we are familiar enough with the material to recall it. It is too late to find out that you can only recognize the data on the day.

Again, some test questions are in the form of selective response and open-ended questions.

Open-ended. A common unit of electrical resistance is called the. . . .

Selective response. A common unit of electrical resistance is called the amp, volt, watt, ohm (tick the answer).

The second form is much easier than the first and this illustrates the difference between recognition and recall.

In ordinary life situations as distinct from examinations it may be important to build in repetitions to ensure that instructions are recalled. Devices such as check-lists are useful as reminders of a set of instructions, especially if they are not necessarily logically linked in some sequence.

Transfer

But exact recall is very rarely of any use, except in examinations. Bartlett made this point in his book *The Mind at Work and Play*. What is wanted is that people will abstract something from one situation to be used in another situation which is often quite different.

This insistence on exact recall results in problems which could easily be avoided if the importance of transfer was recognized.

I was once invigilating an H.N.C. examination and I noticed that a candidate was very carefully screening his paper with his left hand from a person who had his back to him. So carefully was he doing this that I got suspicious and turned up the palm of his left hand. Across the palm were written the formulae he wanted. Now I hardly blame the man, I would rather blame the system which has put him in this ridiculous situation.

Again, I saw a person standing outside an examination hall studying very carefully some material on a single sheet of paper. As soon as the door opened he dropped the paper, rushed inside and picked up a clean piece of paper and wrote the material down on it. He had taken no material aid into the room, but I'd like to bet that in his anxiety to remember, he had forgotten some things, even over a distance of 3 yards.

Continuing this argument. Suppose I say to you, "What is the radius of a sphere of volume 30 in³?" What do you do?

You first have to remember the formula for the volume of a sphere $V = 4/3\pi r^3$.

You then have to transpose this formula for r:

$$r = \sqrt[3]{\left(\frac{3V}{4\pi}\right)}.$$

You then have to substitute figures and using logs or the slide rule, calculate the answer.

The exercise is designed to see whether you can make use of the formula by transposing and calculating—but you cannot start unless you can remember the formula, and if you fail to remember I cannot test your ability to transpose.

Why then do we not say If the formula for the volume of a sphere is

$$V = 4/3\pi r^3,$$

then find the radius of a sphere of volume 30 in³.

You might argue that it is important to remember formulae; but if you have forgotten a formula in real life you look it up in a book or consult an authority, and if you are using it so often that you are repeating it daily, then you have no need to look it up because repetition has stamped it in.

Please do not test *exact recall*; concern yourself very much with *transfer of experiences*.

This following example illustrates transfer vividly.

A lad came home from a secondary grammar school at the end of his first term, with a physics exam paper. At the bottom of the page was a question which said, "Find the area of this figure"— (depicting a semi-circle).

His mother said to him, "How did you do that?"

Boy: I drew it on some squared paper and counted up the little squares and little bits of squares and told them how many little squares it was.

(This, of course, is fundamental: "You always measure something with a bit of the same sort of thing for which you have a name." He had used this principle, but I guess he was marked wrong.)

But his mother wasn't satisfied.

Mother: Didn't you realize this was a semicircle?
Boy: Yes.
Mother: How do you find the area of a circle?
Boy: πr^2 (Just about within the range of this age group, but only just).
Mother: How do you find the area of a semicircle, then?
Boy: You divide by 2.
Mother: Then why didn't you do that here?
Boy: Well, this is physics—not mathematics.

This is a perfect example of the failure to transfer. It had never occurred to the lad (and what is more important no one had given him the idea) that this formula could be used anywhere. There was no transfer.

This illustrates what occurs in many great discoveries. A person sees a link between two things which have appeared to be different and, as soon as he does so, information learnt in one situation can be transferred to the other—a major discovery is made—the penny drops.

It is transfer which is the important thing about memory and if this is to take place we must notice *similarities* whereas biologically we tend to notice *differences* and the unusual. Bartlett* in making this point argues that we must adapt teaching methods to draw attention to the possibilities of similarities if we want to encourage transfer.

This may account for one of the differences between programmed texts and ordinary teaching. The teacher of experience is often spending a deal of time on looking for and making illustrations to help transfer of experience, and this may not be measured

* F. C. Bartlett, *The Mind at Work and Play*, Allen & Unwin, pp. 140–1, pp. 115, 118.

when making comparative trials between methods with or without programmed texts.

I remember making nitrobenzene in the chemical laboratory at school. I tested its properties and poured the remainder down the sink. I then looked up the list to see what was the next preparation and found it was to make a chemical using nitrobenzene.

I went into the stores looking for the bottle of commercial nitrobenzene and noticed that it was nearly empty and, "helpful like", said to the teacher, "Have we got to use the nitrobenzene in the stores because the bottle is nearly empty?"

"Of course you don't", he replied, "you use the stuff you made last week. What have you done with that?"

"I poured it down the sink", I said.

"What did you do that for?" he replied.

I nearly told him: "If you had said to me, 'What are you preparing?' I would have said, 'I am preparing nitrobenzene.' If you had said to me, 'What are you testing the properties of?' I would have said, 'I am testing the properties of nitrobenzene'. But I did not think that the stuff in my flask was the same as that in the bottle. That was proper nitrobenzene made by a manufacturing chemist. I had just been following instructions in a book —working to a recipe—no transfer to real life."

It was a useful lesson to learn.

Imagery

Different people recall, using different kinds of imagery:

Some can hear the tune going through their head all day—
audiles.

Some can see the thing in its position on a sheet of paper—
visiles.

Some memorize finger positions and progressions in music
—*motiles*.

This means that in making the initial communication we need to range the senses to allow for preferences of certain individuals for certain kinds of recall. This, in teaching, reinforces the appeal to use training aids.

Problem V—Chain Communication

Almost imperceptibly we are moving now into the passing on of information received in one situation to another situation and, of course, come face to face with the major communication problem of *chain communication*.

What happens when we pass information down a number of links in a chain of communication?

Let us examine the following example:

Suppose I draw the following object on a piece of paper and show it to A, take it away and then ask A to draw what he saw: I take A's copy, show it to B, remove A's copy and ask B to draw what he saw—and so on, C, D, . . ., X. What comes out at X?

Original

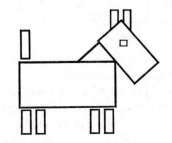

What happens?

One of the first things I do is to name the object, i.e. I rationalize the communication.

Suppose I think it is a dog. Then I draw a dog. But a dog has curves and eyes and ears, and by the time I have drawn these things, what comes out can look like this:

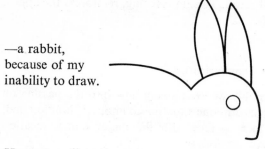

—a rabbit,
because of my
inability to draw.

Hence two distortions:

First, I *rationalize*—I say "What he means is this".

Secondly, I tried to draw a dog, but because of my inability it appears more like a rabbit, i.e. lack of skill in the medium. Thirdly, the individual might say "Not interested—don't want to listen", i.e. resistance to change.

Thus at least three classes of distortion can arise at any stage, due to:

(a) rationalization;
(b) lack of skill in the medium;
(c) resistance to change;

and these are the problems which I have to solve if I want to minimize distortion in chain communication.

In order to avoid (a) tell him the basic principles operating, e.g. this is a dog drawn in squares and rectangles only. He now avoids curves and the rabbit, but he might draw a big dog, a little dog, or a short and fat kind, or a long and thin type—I have not controlled these variables—only dog and squares and rectangles.

More generally this principle says, "Never give an instruction only—always give an instruction and a reason" (see also p. 20).

In order to avoid (b) the solution is training in the use of the medium, i.e. writing, drawing, speaking.

In order to avoid (c) we need to revert to our chapter on attitude change and involve the person in decision making by first getting him to admit there is a problem and then inviting him to comment on outline proposals offered to meet the problem.

Some industrial practices and procedures throw additional light on this problem of chain communication.

At one time we wanted to devise a system for getting modifications in car specifications to each person holding a copy of the specification. This often meant altering just one line only on a large sheet.

First suggestion. Tell the man concerned over the phone to make the alteration concerned.

Specification office: "Jack! Part No. . . . modified—4 off instead of 6—4 in. long instead of $3\frac{1}{2}$ in. Made by X and X Ltd."

Jack: "O.K. Bill. I've made a note; busy at the moment, but will see it goes in."

He forgets, often because he really is very busy and the next time he or his staff order they are wrong.

Reject this method.

Second suggestion. Send someone round to make the alterations personally.

This doesn't work because of individual idiosyncrasies. "Did I put a 4 or a 6?" Have you ever locked the back door and then gone along to check that you had?

Third suggestion. Type a lot of single lines on a sheet, duplicate this, cut them off, dispatch the strips to be stuck into the specification to cover the alteration. What happens? People accumulate these at the front of the specification (too busy) and then fail to check for a modification when using the specification. How many of us really use the "erratum" printed at the front of some books? The book is wrong without these modifications.

Final solution. Reproduce the whole page incorporating the line under consideration. Take it round to the individuals concerned. Unbolt the specification, exchange the appropriate page, and get a signature for it.

This apparent waste of paper illustrates the size of this problem of chain communication.

This central duplication of data also illustrates an important point of procedure.

It has been common to question the commercial practice of reproducing a fair number of carbon copies of orders, etc. But if we really look into this we can see that if the same document is circulated to several departments for each department to abstract what it wants and then pass on to the next user, it is obvious that no one will know what each department has got. But if my secretary makes a mistake on the original, of which there are several carbon copies for the departments, then I know what mistake everyone has got in his carbon copy. The real point to challenge is: Do all these departments need this copy? Let us pay attention to the circulation list and not despise central duplication.

Broadcast systems have been recommended as aids to chain communication problems and the following example will illustrate some of the main points to be found here.

The superintendent of a factory of over 20,000 people wanted to convey the same message to everyone. He called together the staff on the day shift in the staff canteen and spoke through a microphone to the assembled group. The first mistake he made was to choose lunch time for this event. People will not necessarily object to a meeting before lunch, or after lunch in working time, but during lunch time they are interested in food and will be irritated by interruptions in feeding habits. He failed to observe the principle that people will pay attention to things which affect their basic needs. Thus only a few listened—many criticized.

At the same time the talk was relayed to the separate canteens on the production groups. But here, as soon as the superintendent started to speak, the work people started beating their plates with knives and forks and nothing could be heard. The same talk was also recorded and played back on the afternoon and night shifts, with the same result.

The superintendent thought that he had spoken the same words to 20,000 people. If more than a dozen in the "front row of the stalls" heard him, that was about all. And the main reason—

faulty timing and the impatience of the workers with the exploitation of the broadcast system, typified by the epithet "Broadcasting superintendent".

Thus if you have a valuable device for large scale transmission of material:

(a) remember timing and people's basic needs;
(b) do not use it for trivial purposes—earn respect as the BBC radio has so clearly done in aiming at quality and integrity.

Problem VI—Feedback (Control aspect of communication)

At any stage in the communication loop the initiating agency may want to know the state of affairs and to estimate how well the communications have gone over. In order to do this there must be some *feedback*.

There are a number of important principles which can govern this area of the testing of the efficiency of communications. These were first suggested on pp. 49, 50 viz.:

(a) If I give you an instruction and you repeat the instruction to me (word perfect even) it does not follow that you understand it. But, on the other hand, if you repeat my instruction but use your own words and not mine, I know you understand me.

Thus the first test of communication is: *Expression in own words* and *not* repetition of original words (occasionally you may prefer the original wording, but if you do, show that you are quoting).

(b) If I give you an instruction and you engage in an appropriate activity, I know you have understood me, but I need to be there to see the action or its products, i.e. I cannot afford to be aloof from the people I supervise.

Thus the second test of communication is: *Appropriate action*.

(c) If I illustrate things to you from my experience and you illustrate them back to me from your experience, I know you understand me, but if, on the other hand, you repeat my illustration I do not know whether you understand me or not.

Thus the third test of communication is: *Expression in own illustration*.

For this reason we used to say to course members on the old

B.I.M. Management Diploma Course, "If you reproduce roughly what was said on the course you will get about 60 per cent of the marks, but if you illustrate these same points from your own experience, you will get 100 per cent of the marks because this is a guarantee that what was discussed on the course is transferring to your life situation.

This feedback area is probably one of the biggest problem areas in the field of communication. I believe that some supervisors do not report back to their superiors because they think this is a sign of weakness, i.e. that they cannot cope. But if supervisors do not report back, then policies initiated by higher management in all good faith, can be out of touch with reality on the shop/office floor and will not be altered because higher management will not receive information which shows the necessity.

No electronic device is sensitive to changing conditions without a feedback. We are no better than an electronic device. This carries as a corollary that aloofness is unrealistic in human communication networks.

Feedback is the vital element in teaching situations and the difference between the professional paper and the lesson is in the degree of interaction between course member and lecturer. It is important to look at the group to get evidence of reactions in the form of gestures and facial contortions; and so the instructional situation is best described as a teaching–learning situation in which the teacher, other members of the group, and the individual (who for the moment is our concern) interact to maximum advantage.

In the normal everyday contact it can be seen therefore that for feedback purposes and, for the possibility of using many channels of communication:

(a) face-to-face contact is easily the best;
(b) the telephone comes next; and
(c) the written communication is the worst.

The diagram on p. 120 (Fig. 11) summarizes the classes of problem described in the communication loop.

CHAPTER 6

Personality and the Implications
of Personality Traits in Selection
and the Teaching–Learning Situation

Definition

The word "personality" has quite a variety of usages e.g.:

He is a *striking* personality—physical implications.
He has a *scintillating* personality—intellectual implications.
He has an *aggressive* personality
He has a *retiring* personality
$\left.\right\}$ emotional implications.
He has *no* personality—impossible situation.

These all imply aspects of a whole, but a common usage separates personality from physical and intellectual characteristics. Allport* surveyed this field and produced something of the order of fifty usages. This means then that there is likely to be considerable confusion over the field of study unless we define our usage of the term reasonably precisely. The following line of approach to a definition satisfies a great many of the points I wish to make.

If you were faced with identical twins you would be likely to give an instruction to one and complain to the other because it was not carried out. In other words as far as you are concerned you would not be able to discriminate; they would not be distinct personalities. But as you got to know them better, sooner or later you would notice a slight difference between them. One moves

* G. W. Allport, *Personality: A Psychological Interpretation*, New York, 1937, Constable, pp. 27, 50. See also G. W. Allport, *Pattern and Growth in Personality*, Holt, Rinehart & Winston, 1961.

slightly differently or has a fleck in the hair (acquired or otherwise), or speaks slightly differently, and then you would be able to discriminate. Thus personality has something to do with these differences. Accordingly it is suggested that *personality is the sum of the qualities which distinguish an individual*, implying that a quality is no use as a personality trait unless it does distinguish people in a given setting.

But we cannot stop here because we know that the same person can exhibit different personalities in different situations.

> "He's a saint on Sunday and a devil in the week."
> "I wouldn't have believed it was the same person."
> "He's like a fish out of water."
> "He's strictly honest in his business dealings but he tells a few white lies when necessary."
> "He's bone idle except on the football field."

What we assess of a person at work may not be what we will see at home, or in a pub, theatre, church, and the like. In other words the personality of an individual is not necessarily a fixed thing, it varies with environment.

Accordingly a working definition could be: *personality is the sum of the qualities which distinguish a person in the environment in which you find him.* This means physical characteristics, intellectual characteristics, and emotional characteristics—all seen against a background of the environment in which we find him.*

The variable factor of the environmental setting of course accounts for some of our difficulties in interviewing for posts. We see an "interview personality" and what we are really trying to

---

* Burt writing in the *British Journal of Educational Psychology* **17**, 107 (1945): "Personality is the entire system of relatively permanent tendencies, both physical and mental, that are distinctive of a given individual and determine his characteristic adjustments to his material and social circumstances."

Allport, ibid., **16**, 65 (January 1946) accepts this in its essential features as being in accord with his own definition quoted on page 47 of his book, *Personality—A Psychological Interpretation*, 1937: "Since there is no such thing as a wrong definition of any term, if it is supported by usage, it is evident that, no one, neither theologian, the philosopher, the jurist, the sociologist, the man in the street, nor the psychologist, can monopolize 'personality'."

assess is a "work-situation personality". This means, of course, that it is not a bad idea to try to make the interview situation a little like the work situation and, for example, conduct a 1 : 1 interview on the job, actually moving around, discussing real situations which arise spontaneously (not simulated ones).

This kind of definition will also make sense of some of the modern approaches to leadership. I have noticed, for example, that it is not necessarily the man who leads the discussion in the conference room in courses for the Steel Company of Wales who leads the singing in the pub. In fact it is quite an interesting exercise to try to decide beforehand who will lead the singing. On the other hand, I must admit I have met a man who played for the British Lions at Rugby Football, who was also a Ph.D. and did not take a back seat in the singing either. But yet, again, I know a man who, when at school, beat everyone easily in scientific pursuits, was captain of the school at cricket and football, was very well received socially, but could not (or would not) plane a piece of wood straight to save his life.

This variable aspect of the concept of personality is of vital importance because a belief in the fixed nature of personality traits has led, erroneously, to systems of rating qualities of behaviour like industriousness, initiative, dexterity, and even intelligence on the assumption that once assessed they would be tenable in any situation. They are tenable only for the situations in which they are assessed, and only repeated tendencies can establish their probability of application to other situations. We will return to this important point later when we look at the possible use of personality traits, as mentioned above, i.e. attitudes— as indicators of interest areas. In the meantime let us emphasize that aspect of the definition of personality which stresses

relative to the environment.

Man and His Environment
Systematic Plan

In view of the previous argument, if we want a systematic plan for looking at personality, then we must start with man and his environment. But we realize that when we meet a person for the first time, the first thing we notice is what he looks like, i.e. physical characteristics (unless we cannot see him). It will be later that we shall be trying to assess him as a *mental* specimen. On the mental side we may be concerned with his *intellectual* make-up, but on other occasions with the *emotional* characteristics he exhibits, and, in pondering on these, as we do sometimes, we may wonder to what extent these are *innate* or *acquired*.

Thus we see the beginnings of a systematic way of studying personality. We consider man in an environment of some sort (he does not exist in a vacuum); we consider his physical and mental make-up, the intellectual and emotional aspects, and argue about what is acquired (learnt) and what innate. This leads to something like the N.I.I.P. Seven-point Plan for Selection (National Institue of Industrial Psychology). Figure 12 suggests this plan for looking at man and his environment and automatically defines terms. It can be used to look at the demands which a job makes on a person and it can be used to study the characteristics of the candidate for the job. I am not at all sure that it is possible always to distinguish between what is innate and what acquired and so tend to use a broader plan of job study:

What *physical demands* does the job make on a person?
What *intellectual demands* does the job make on a person?
What *emotional satisfactions* does it offer him?
What *special environmental circumstances* do we need to take into consideration?

Nevertheless, for the sake of teasing out some of the problems involved in personality assessment, let us consider the items on the plan listed in Fig. 12 with general, but not necessarily exclusive, reference to selection.

Personality and Selection—General Considerations
Physical Traits
We can list here such characteristics as flat feet, weak heart, cauliflower ear, red hair, blue eyes, unusual dexterity, unusual

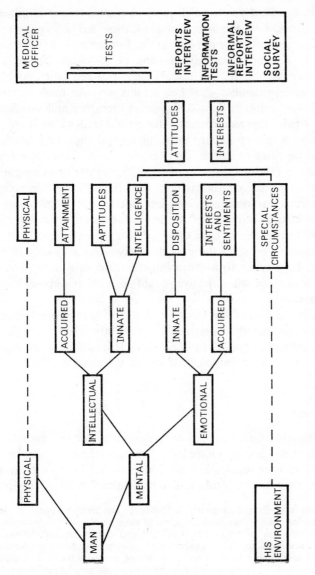

FIG. 12. Man and his environment. Illustrating selection methods.

strength, excellent voice, height and physique, colour blindness, sense defects, and the like. Some of these are occupationally significant and some are not important. For example, a policeman cannot be flat-footed or have a weak heart—more flippantly a cauliflower ear might be a qualification and red hair and blue eyes an embarrassment—but height; this we have made occupationally significant. It is listed in career literature and standards are set. Again, a person cannot enter certain trades if he is colour blind, and a mining deputy must have good sight and hearing.

When we come to things like dexterity we run into difficulties. It is easy to fall into the trap of regarding dexterity as an entity rather than a quality of behaviour. Tests have shown that people are dextrous in some activities but not in others involving a different kind of movement.* In fact you cannot buy a dexterity test; you have really to have one made for the situation. In other words there is no such thing as dexterity; it is a quality of behaviour. It is better to avoid using the word as a noun, but to use it rather as an adjective qualifying behaviour—*dextrous* behaviour.

(This is the first of the traps we shall mention about this tendency to assume that personality traits are fixed identifiable entities, instead of *qualities* of *behaviour*. If we think of the adjective we do not make mistakes. If we use the noun we do.)

Attainment

Attainment is listed as acquired intellectual mental characteristics of man, and implies all we have ever learnt. Learning has many associations with scholastic establishments, but here we mean all we have ever learnt inside and outside the formal educational

---

* Vernon and Parry, *Personnel Selection in the British Forces*, p. 167. "The 'naming fallacy' has been the bane of vocational psychology—witness the ubiquitous use of 'manual dexterity', 'visual discrimination', 'attention to detail', and the like. Factor analysis investigations indeed show that there is so little overlapping between different tests of dexterity that it is doubtful whether it should be credited with any general and independent existence."

system—trade knowledge, knowledge of people, properties of matter, and the like.

Now if we look at our policeman we can see that we can set standards for attainment levels. He must be able to read and write—but how well? As well as George Bernard Shaw? Must he know the Calculus? The answer is, "No!" And some career booklets say, "Good A-stream secondary modern school level"—whatever that might mean.

Must the policeman know anything about the law? The answer is, "Yes if he practising, but not necessarily if he is an entrant," because we are proposing to put him through a training experience to put that matter right. And so it depends sometimes on whether we are thinking of a person to do the job straight away or whether he is to go through a training experience to do the job later on.

Now we are making a lot of mistakes in current practice in this field of attainments. We are using public examination results, never designed for the purpose, to set target levels for attainments in selection, and almost invariably we are setting our targets too high.

A man once asked my advice about the selection of potential secretaries to heads of departments in the firm. He complained of high labour turnover.

I asked him to outline his procedure and his first statement was, "We ask for 5 O-levels in the G.C.E." I asked, "Why?" (always ask why) and he did not know. But recovering quickly he said, "Good material". Now I know it could be good material, but does he want such material? Because if he over-selects he will get frustrated labour, inefficiency (because attention wanders), and high labour turnover.

What is the real problem? Let us look for a moment at clerical grades.

First the copy typist. Her job is to make a fair copy of a document written in manuscript form or a typed document altered and modified for some purpose. She has to be able to read but not necessarily to spell or punctuate, because these are already done for her (and some bosses take great exception to alterations to spelling and grammatical construction; but if you are using a copy typist to correct your English you are not employing a copy typist). Her main source of satisfaction is work in a regular structured situation, clearly defined. Personal satisfaction is from volume of work, no overtyping, and fair copy—very likely even the layout will be specified for her.

Now the shorthand typist. She takes down phonetically (shorthand or tape) and therefore must be able to spell. Demands on English are higher than for the copy typist. Occasionally she may have to compose a little when the boss gives her a free hand, but now she is moving more towards a secretary. She has some varied situations—can exercise some initiative on layout—more personal contacts.

But what of the secretary? She is a person who is exposed to a whole variety of demands, impacting on her almost simultaneously. She has to create order out of chaos and sometimes satisfy several different people. And so the first characteristic is that she must be prepared and be able to exercise initiative and discretion. She must not expect a structured situation, as is typical of the copy typist. But she must be able to cope with shorthand (or audiotyping) and compose if necessary. The demands on her intellectually are as great as on the shorthand typist, but there is the prime demand to be able to exercise discretion.

My point is that the chief difference between the secretary and the other two classes of clerical labour probably turns on attitude. There is nothing here about G.C.E. O-level mathematics or comparable intellectual attainment levels, and it is likely that the man had missed excellent material in the "Good A-stream secondary modern girl" or "failed G.C.E." The minimum intellectual demand is often lower than we think; but other demands are higher.

Again, labour turnover in the graduate area is often of the order of 50 per cent, and this can well be due to an overstating of the intellectual demands of the job and these high levels not materializing in practice.

It is a mistake to recruit labour which is too good for the job, or to "raise your sights" in view of a bulge in the school population. If the job does not offer the necessary intellectual challenges, then frustration and disillusionment will set in with consequent high labour turnover.

It is important to analyse the intellectual demands realistically and not be blinded by an apparently useful examination qualification usually designed to meet another set of circumstances. If, however, you can show that a particular examination requirement gives evidence of the attainment demands of a particular job, by all means use it. *But do your analysis first.*

Intelligence and Aptitudes

This is the aspect of personality which best illustrates the dangers of generalization and assumption of transfer. We talk as though a person has a quality called intelligence which we can sample in one situation and thereby make a measure/estimate which will apply to another situation. In fact intelligence is an abstraction; all we have evidence of is behaviour and we describe certain kinds of behaviour as intelligent. We make comparisons between people's abilities to make certain kinds of intelligent decision, and this is all we can do. Any mathematical treatment of the data and factor analyses are only ways of presenting data— presenting the test results, but in the end *the only reality is behaviour and our ability to compare performances.** Let us look at this in more detail.

* C. J. C. Earl, *The Study of Society*, Kegan Paul, 1946, ch. x, p. 231. ". . . whatever label we attach to a given test or measure what is in fact being tested or measured is not 'intelligence', 'temperament', 'character" 'emotionality', or any similar abstraction, but behaviour; and behaviour is a function of the personality as a whole. All our tests are, therefore, in the ultimate analysis, tests of personality, though possibly with special reference to one or other of its particular aspects."

We tend to say a person is intelligent if he can follow a complicated instruction. But no one would accept the definition, "Intelligence is the ability to follow a complicated instruction". If a person continually makes the same mistake, e.g. continually bumps his head against a low beam, we say that the person is not very intelligent. Are we saying that, "Intelligence is the ability to profit by previous experience"? Some people would begin to think that this was more like it—but still hesitate.

Let us go further; consider the sequence:

2, 4, 8, 16? What is the next number? (*Ans.:* 32.)

In working this out you will be looking at the relationship between pairs of these numbers, trying alternatives, selecting the common one, and applying that relationship to the last to deduce what was next in sequence. Seeing relationships between elements and using that relationship to deduce the missing item (inductive and deductive reasoning)—this, says Spearman* is intelligence.

Try it now in the form of analysis involving words:

Day : Night,   White: . . . ?

(As *day* is to *night*, so is *white* to . . . ?) (*Ans.:* Black. It could be Negro.)

But our earlier examples had also in mind "following instructions" and "profiting by previous experience" as well.

Again, if we give a person a job to do which he has never seen before and he learns fast, we say he is an intelligent person. Does this mean that intelligence is linked with speed of learning?

If we give a person a complicated job to do and he plans ahead very well, we say he is intelligent. Planning ahead is a measure of intelligence: Is it?

Now it is obvious from these examples that a whole range of different kinds of behaviour are accepted by people as intelligent behaviour. But it would be very difficult to get any one of these accepted as a complete definition of intelligence. Accordingly, avoid the abstraction intelligence and concentrate on *making*

* Spearman, *The Nature of Intelligence and the Principles of Cognition*, 1923.

comparisons between people's abilities to make the kind of intelligent decisions you know are at a premium in the job.

With this proviso in mind it would not matter that people were talking about intelligence when they really meant limited kinds of intelligent behaviour, but the difficulty arises when, at the age of 11+, children are given tests of the type:

2, 4, 8, 16   what is the next number?

Day : Night,   White : . . . ?,

i.e. verbal intelligence tests, and on the basis of this kind of test children in certain kinds of schools are labelled "not very intelligent". (This may not have been the original intention, but it has certainly become actual practice.) Now it is true that unless a person can make intelligent decisions in the sphere of words and numbers, he will not profit from an education in a secondary grammar school, but we cannot say of those who do not—"not very intelligent", because we have no evidence of how intelligently they will match a tool to a job, or handle their social relationships. I am with Dr. C. M. Flemming* when she said in a talk in Newcastle, "You have no right to make judgements about people in areas in which you have made no measurements."

Thus I stick to intelligent behaviour and avoid intelligence. *Define the kind of behaviour you are interested in and make your measures/comparisons in that area.*

Dr. E. Venables (now Lady Venables) reported some useful test scores for engineering apprentices in the *British Journal of Educational Psychology* in 1960. Figure 13 presents some of these results. It shows that when engineering apprentices were given a verbal intelligence test, N.I.I.P. test 33, they did not stand out noticeably in the general population, in fact appeared pretty well as a cross-section of the population. When, however, they were given the non-verbal test, progressive matrices (1947), they stood out exceptionally, as able people. One is inclined to ask, "Well, are these engineers bright lads or are they not?", and the answer seems to be, "It depends on what you measure."

* Speaking to diploma students in the University of Newcastle Institute of Education, 1965.

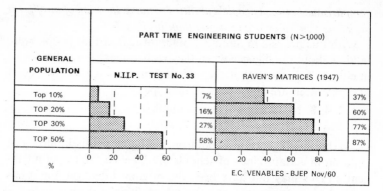

FIG. 13. Performances at verbal (test 33) and non-verbal (matrix) tests compared.

Generally, of course, the engineer rids his problem situations of words and turns them into equations, formulae, and diagrams. It might be that the engineer is not particularly interested in verbal situations but he is interested in the problems involving patterns and diagrams. Thus an interest factor may have complicated the situation.

Now if there is some form of computer system in the form of the brain, we never see its real quality because it operates through some self-interest sieve. Maybe, then, we should drop the word intelligence and think more of aptitude, i.e. limited interest areas in which intelligent decisions are made. Perhaps then we would agree with Professor P. E. Vernon (London Institue of Education) when he says maybe we should call a verbal intelligence test a scholastic aptitude test. I am certainly with him. (If we accept this kind of idea we should attribute to an individual that quality of "brain" of the highest level at which *we have ever observed him perform*—verbal situation, practical or social.)

Disposition

If we look at the work of the biologist we find that he says we can study all living organisms on the plan:

(a) What activities do they pursue to maintain themselves alive?

(b) What activities do they pursue to maintain the species?

If I ask why we bother to stay alive, especially in some of the very difficult conditions we experience, I find people have recourse to phrases like, "Oh, it's natural, I suppose", "It's instinctive", and the like. When pushed a little further a number of people will admit to a belief in three instincts:

Instinct of self-preservation.
Instinct of herd.
Instinct of sex.

William McDougall wanted fourteen instincts, but others disliked the word instinct for people (but would accept it for animals). Accordingly, McDougall changed the word: "What about innate propensities then?" But there is still debate.

A symposium was arranged by the British Psychological Society* on the topic, "Is the doctrine of instincts dead?", and it appeared that whilst we can agree about behaviour we cannot necessarily agree about explanations.

Perhaps then this is the clue. We can all agree that we can produce evidence to demonstrate *curiosity* in people and can establish that if we do not poke our noses into things around us, then sooner or later we shall be at a great disadvantage and might even be killed by that unusual element in our environment (i.e that curiosity is of biological significance in survival). We can also, on introspection, agree that we were not taught to be "nosy", but rather taught by our parents to be "discreetly nosy".

Again I can demonstrate *pugnacity* by frustrating individuals in pursuit of certain goals, and can recall *flight*, i.e. unease in a group when it tends to move away from a very unusual element which suddenly appears in their environment.

It appears then that we have inherited something from pre-

* Is the doctrine of instincts dead? *British Journal of Educational Psychology* vols. 11, 12, 13.

vious generations designed to perpetuate ourselves alive. What this is we can debate, but we can all agree about the behaviour. I propose to designate, whatever it was that we inherited, which is at the back of this behaviour, as *disposition*. This is a William McDougall's term (sum total of instincts). Some people will exhibit a pugnacious disposition; some a curious disposition; and so on.

Interests, i.e., Sentiments and Complexes

When we associate with people and things and ideas, we tend to develop structures of emotions called *sentiments* around these people and things and ideas, and these bias us in certain ways. For example:

If you buy a dog and the next door neighbour buys a dog from the same litter, broadly speaking these two dogs are similar, but in 6 months' time your dog will be better than his. Your dog would wag its tail when it saw you. It doesn't follow that the next door neighbour's would. If your dog steals the beef steak from next door. "Well, that's natural. What do you expect dogs to do? They should put it away safely." But if their dog steals your beef steak. "It's time they did something about that animal. It's out of control."

Notice *things* we have associated with are not regarded in the same way as things we have not associated with.

Again—if your son or young relative gets into trouble with the Police: "Well, it's only high spirits really, you know! But it's time they locked up that irresponsible young devil at the end of the road—he's a menace!"

Notice *people* you have associated with are not regarded in the same way as people you have not associated with.

Yet again—long after everyone else has proved *your idea* to be wrong, you are still holding on to it because *you* thought of it.

In this way, then, we form sentiments from normal life experiences and we can develop complexes from unusual experiences. If we put sentiments and complexes together we have a general classification called *interests*.

Thus interests are acquired structures, developed as a result of our previous experiences. They bias us in favour of certain kinds of situation.

Special Circumstances

If we were looking for a sales representative, we would look for a man with:

Good *physical* appearance, good presence, good voice.

Good trade *knowledge*; cannot be faulted in his knowledge of the product.

Good *social intelligence*; makes good decisions in handling people.

A man who is *tenacious* (comes back again and again; can take a setback), but not pugnacious.

Interested in selling and the kind of situations surrounding selling.

But you would not give him the job if his wife objected to him being away from home at night. Notice, then, a man may meet all reasonable requirements for a job but may be faulted on the last one—the ability to fit in with the *special circumstances* affecting the work. In this case either the job would wreck the family or the family would wreck the job.

It is no use taking on a man who cannot work nights for domestic reasons, e.g. dependent relatives, if shift working is a necessary part of the job. Again, certain jobs demand a degree of mobility and irregular working hours; some demand that you must meet the security regulations and some demand that you can drive a car and have a clean licence.

Recently I heard of a research appointment which was made and when it was completed and confirmed, someone discovered that the new appointee could not drive a car and this was essential for the job. In other words someone had forgotten that in addition to meeting the physical, intellectual, and emotional demands of a job, special circumstances arising from the environment of the work situation also had to be complied with.

There are occasions, of course, where certain privilege clauses apply to a job. These should appear appropriately in the special circumstances area, e.g. other things being equal, appointment should be from within the firm. Yet again I have known people be selected because they could fit a special circumstances clause—they could play a trombone and we were short in the band, or, better still, they happened to be particularly good as a left half.

Now looking at these aspects of personality and the comments made, it is not suggested that personality is the sum total of these characteristics. These are rather aspects of a complex called personality. They interact to produce the behaviour we see exhibited. For example, we never see a person's disposition. In any situation the prime impulse operating may be one of aggression, but what we would actually see would be the prime impulse modified by an intelligent evaluation of the situation or by the operation of some sentiment, producing compromise behaviour and the attitudes which we adopt as appropriate to the circumstances obtaining.

However, such a plan for studying personality can be employed for selection purposes and the N.I.I.P. seven-point plan has a well-established reputation in this field. I would simplify this a little because of the confusion between innate and acquired characteristics and would use four main categories as mentioned before (p. 144).

Personality and Selection in Particular

Job Description

The first task in a selection procedure is to describe the work situation and activities involved, i.e. *describe the job*.

This is not necessarily easy to do, because a job presupposes that the individual returns to a given class of activities sufficiently regularly for this to be recognized. It also presupposes we know the best method of doing the job. We know neither of these in many cases. In fact the more variety there is in the work the more difficult it is to define the job. For this reason it might be more appropriate to define the *prime functions* exercised rather than the *specific tasks done.** This gives us a *job description.*

Job Analysis

The next task is to say when the individual is exercising these functions:

(a) What *physical demands* does the work make on the person?
(b) What *intellectual demands* does the work make on the person?
(c) What *emotional satisfactions* does it offer him?
(d) What *special circumstances* does the employer insist he complies with?

(Or a slightly more extensive set of questions if the seven-point plan is used.) This operation is called *job analysis* and *yields the specification of the person we are looking for.*

Assessing the Candidate

The next phase is to assess to what extent the different candidates match up to this specification using the same plan for studying personality.

Profiles

This scheme is straightforward enough and implies no ambiguity and has led to the impression that a nice neat profile of demands could be matched by a nice neat profile for the applicant,

---

* If you select and train for tasks you risk redundancy. If you select and train for function this leads to versatility.

and the best fit is the required person. In actual practice, however, precision of this sort is out of the question in view of the crude nature of the measuring devices available and the difficulties of describing the work situations. It is to be expected therefore that the edges of the profiles will be considerably blurred. With this proviso in mind, let us now look at real practice.

Practical Considerations

Selection in Practice

Some selection procedures are extensive affairs with the use of test material, interviews, and other procedures combined. I propose to look at various types of procedure commonly in use and the possible introduction of one or two new developments.

Use of tests

I remember being told by a senior official, "I've no room for your box of tricks", but on pressing the individual further, discovered that he did his selection by asking questions of his own devising. But what are these but tests? They are tests of his own invention and might well be very good tests. I have a great deal of respect for people's own tests provided they have thought a good deal about them; but of course there are tests devised by other people, and some of these, too, are useful. But one thing is clear, everybody uses tests, paper and pencil, oral, or practical *because no one can make judgements about another person unless that person does something*.

Appendix II sets out a complete selection procedure illustrating the use of tests, much of which is of practical use today. The reader interested in this field is recommended to consider some of the devices listed.

Selection by interview

Selection interview can be on a 1 : 1 basis or by a small panel interviewing one person at a time or by a panel observing and rating all the candidates interacting together. There are, of course, other methods, or combinations of methods, but for the moment let us consider the *panel interview*.

Number on panel

I am a little opposed to the 1 : 1 interview (unless it is conducted on the job) because I realize that if I ask a candidate a challenging question he can tell me:

(a) What he thinks I want to know.
(b) What he thinks it conventional to say.
(c) What he really believes.

If, however, I ask questions indirectly, I am more likely to get what he believes. If, therefore, I get the answer to my question while he is talking to someone else, then I can get nearer to reality. Consequently I prefer a small panel.

But how many should be on this small panel and who should they be?

In my opinion, the first person to be on a panel should be the *immediate consumer* (i.e. the person who is going to supervise and use the individual being selected). If he is not on the panel he should have been very much concerned with the job analysis, since he is the person who knows most about the actual work situation.

The second person to be on a panel should be someone to represent conditions of service, e.g. personnel officer, registrar, member of establishments branch, secretary of the company, as appropriate to the appointment level. The reason for this is that someone has to be able to state, with authority, conditions of service and any help available, say in transition problems, superannuation, and the like.

The third person needs to be someone with a bigger view of the organization than the immediate consumer, and he could, very appropriately, be the chairman of the panel. This, I think, would be enough; but, of course, some organizations demand representation and this sometimes means more people.

Procedure

Having got our panel, now how do we proceed? I have known panel members to assemble, to be engaged in general conversation, when someone has come along and said: "Can we start now? They're waiting outside." At this stage I have heard people say, "What are we looking for?" Perhaps we are lucky that they got as far as thinking about this before the candidates went in, but generally, of course, this is a disgrace. Someone should have done a job analysis and this is what we are looking for; but more

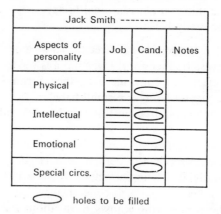

Fig. 14.

than this, we already know something about the persons outside the door because either they have applied for the job or we have asked them to come up for consideration and we know them in the firm. Thus before Jack Smith comes in for interview we need to decide, "What we do know about him already and what are the gaps in our knowledge of how he fits our specification" (from the job analysis). The important thing at this stage is to decide what we need to find out (i.e. what we do not know) and to agree in the panel as to how this should be done.

For example, for Jack Smith, we might agree that we need to know (Fig. 14):

(a) How well he can express himself in the English language using say a five-point (A–E) rating.
(b) Why the discrepancy in his employment record?
(c) What are his chief work interests (not hobbies)?
(d) How mobile he is.

The chairman could allocate Mr. X to assess the use of English language on the five-point rating (see later for use of ratings). He could tell Mr. Y to check the discrepancy in the employment record, and he himself might undertake the mobility question and the work interests. The point is everyone now knows what has to be done; everyone has a task and the interview does not stop until everyone is satisfied because otherwise we will not know how well Jack Smith matches our specification obtained from the job analysis.

Jack Smith is now introduced with minimum fuss and no display of power or arrogance. (We want the truth—do not play games however clever you might think them. If you play serious games, make sure he knows the rules, or otherwise you are wasting everyone's time.)

The chairman needs to help the man to settle in and a broad question like, "I see you worked for 'So-and-So' for 10 years, will you tell us something about it?", can be very useful in this respect (i.e. let the man talk himself steady by describing a situation he knows well). But it can also be useful to X who has to rate how he can express himself. The candidate thinks he is describing something to the chairman, but he is providing X with a natural situation to observe and rate and not one deliberately aimed to impress him and obtain a high rating. At the same time this question can bracket the area of discrepancy in the record, and with a few judicious followers Y, too, can solve his problem. (Thus the general question can provide a means for answering detailed questions.)

But from time to time the chairman may need to know how his colleagues are proceeding and so the open question, "Mr. Y, would you like to ask the candidate any more questions?" can supply him with the answer. If Mr. *Y* says, "No thank you, I'm perfectly satisfied", it means his hole is plugged, but if he says, "Well, there are one or two points I would like to make", then it suggests that he wants questions to cover the discrepancy in Jack Smith's record as fully as possible.

Alec Rodger* of Birkbeck once remarked to the effect that the interview is notoriously unreliable, but that it was so much part of our traditional set-up that he doubted that we could get rid of it and accordingly the obvious thing to do was to make it work. *Plan your interview beforehand.*

Now when Bill Thomas comes in for interview there are some of the same kind of things we want to know and some are different—so discuss his case as well.

It is obvious that emergencies in interviewing do arise, e.g. "Look, Jack, I've been called away to *Z* and was due as a member of an interview panel at 2.30 p.m. Sit in for me, will you, and do what you can." It is on these occasions that a brief job analysis and interview form are invaluable, especially if preceded by briefing before each candidate is interviewed.

Regarding procedure, remember that the candidate will not do anything until you tell him and he must not be left high and dry at the end. Does he wait? Are you writing, or what? Remember also that he is considering you as well as you considering him. Let him ask questions as well. Encourage him to talk. (Three main questions each for a panel of three, with the interplay, will be enough for a 30-minute interview.)

Halo effect

Now what are the big problems and some of the small snags?

First, the *halo effect*. If a person walks into an interview room and his physical appearance and bearing are excellent, approve this in the appropriate space on the interview sheet (if this is important), but do not let this prejudice your judgement later when you realize he is not doing too well on some of your more demand-

* Alec Rodger writing in *Occupational Psychology*, **26**, 106 (April 1952). See also Vernon and Parry, *Personnel Selection in the British Forces*, 1949.

ing questions. (Well, he did not do too well, but he looks smart doesn't he?) Similarly do not let political or social pressures influence your judgement.

The best safeguard against the halo effect is to do a job analysis. Deal with each aspect separately, and if you have to assess a quality, consider some systematic approach to rating.

Rating scales

Say to yourself: Does this person *stand out* with respect to this *quality*? (Fig. 15).

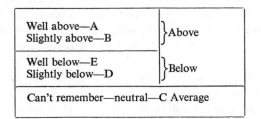

FIG. 15.

The reason for this recommendation is that biologically we notice the unusual, so we will know whether a person is better than or worse than but will have difficulty in assessing average—*rate average by omission.*

Standards

But when we recommend that you ask yourself, "Does this person stand out?", you will say, "Stand out with respect to what?"

When we interview a group of people in a given category for the first time, we are obliged to rate with respect to the candidates appearing at the time. But when we meet a new set, we rate with respect to the present group and our recollection of the previous group. When we meet a third group, we rate with respect to the present group, our recollection of the second group, and our fainter impressions of the first group. Now while it is not really as simple as that, we will gradually form a general impression of the level of candidates expected to turn up at a given level. We develop a norm for that level. (Notice—not all the world—just that level.) In fact it is quite common for a panel member to say, "We've got a good lot this time"—justifying why he has not used D or E or, "We have a poor lot this time", i.e. no A's or B's. If we accept this natural tendency on the part of the assessor to rate with respect to his wider experience, we shall keep fairly near to a current common standard instead of varying erratically according to the chance levels of intake at the time.

The five-point rating is a very useful qualitative scale, but avoid turning it into a numerical scale. A is better than B and B is better than C, but not necessarily by the same amount. (On a numerical scale 5 is better than 4 and 4 is better than 3 by the same amount.)

In interviewing, avoid giving marks for separate qualities and totalling them. Even if the marks for the separate qualities are comparable, you will still be letting one good quality compensate for a poor one, and this is not what you want (however convenient the system is administratively). *You are smoothing out the very variance you want.*

Good English and bad arithmetic can never be average at both.

Set a minimum standard in each area separately. Some areas will be "Go" and "No go" only, e.g. can he meet the security regulations; but his ability to express himself orally might be B on a five-point rating (A–E), for the usual run of intake in that category of labour.

Assessing Interests

In the previous example of Jack Smith, the chairman had undertaken to assess work interests. How can he do this?

First distinguish between work interests and hobbies. (Hobbies can be of supporting value, but not usually of directive value.)

The following remarks apply to the assessment of *work inter-*

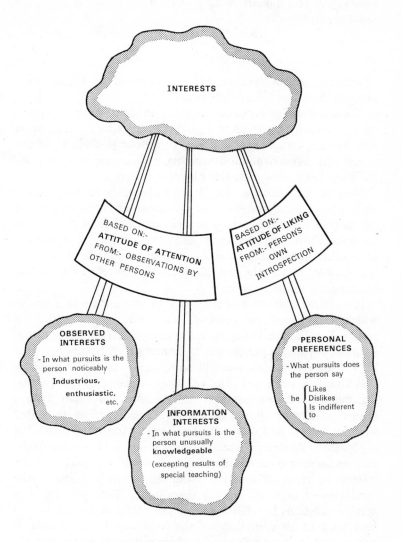

FIG. 16 Assessment of interests.

ests. Figure 16 summarizes the approach but let us examine each point separately.

Observed interests—testimonials and references

When we say of another, "He is interested in *X*", on what grounds do we make the statement?

The first line of evidence could be that we had observed him in the past continually returning to a given class of activity. That is, we had noted a certain persistence in behaviour (associated in our minds with terms like industriousness, enthusiasm, initiative, and the like). Let us designate this observed interests.

Now in the interview situation we obviously cannot observe such interest for a stranger (I do not know any firm who has a big display room into which it turns its candidates in order to record in which area they settle) and so we are obliged to find out from other people who have observed the candidate in the past, i.e. observed him in the real life situation. Hence the question of testimonials and references.

Now to me a testimonial is a general statement about a person which, because of our previous statements on the nature of personality, I argue, is impossible to complete. The reason is that I cannot say that a person will be honest (in all situations); that he will be industrious (he will sometimes); that he will show initiative (on occasion). He *will vary*. Accordingly a general statement, i.e. a testimonial, is not tenable. But I can write a limited statement about an individual in relation to stated situations. That is, I can write a *reference*. Accordingly, ask the candidate to submit the names of some referees. Now write to the referees sending them details of the job at stake. In fact send the referees as much information about the job as you sent to the candidate—a copy of the job description. Then you can ask specific questions in relation to that job area and the referee will look back in his experience of the candidate for those bits of evidence which have a forward-looking viewpoint on the job. He thus writes a limited statement (which might include terms like industriousness, initiative, and the like in relation to that situation), but not a general statement.

When people ask me to write them a testimonial I never do. I say, "I met this person in this kind of situation where he was doing this and this and this, and in these kinds of situations, I found him to be so and so and so." In other words I write a limited statement, which is all I can do in view of the possible changing nature of personality from situation to situation.

Information interests

The second line of evidence on interests is that I have noticed that the individual is unusually knowledgeable about certain things. Designate this *information interests*.

This is the basis of the information test which in effect says, "If a person is interested in X he will be knowledgeable over and above the average about X." The assumption is that in attending to X (because of his interest), he has acquired knowledge about X and has retained this because it is useful to him in pursuing his interest in this field.

Thus if I say to a person, "Which way do the teeth on a hacksaw blade point: upright; away from the handle; towards the handle?" then I am trying to discover the individual who has used a hacksaw, probably broken a blade and has had to replace it and in doing so, has had to find which way to put the new one in, and because all this is useful to him, has retained the knowledge.

Twenty such small questions are useful in selecting potential mechanical apprentices.* In fact in the mining industry we were not able to discriminate between potential electrical and mechanical engineers on aptitude tests, but we were able to do this with interest tests of the information type. These, because of their content, can be geared precisely to a trade.

The content of these tests should include knowledge of tools, materials, processes, conditions of work, relationships, prospects,

* Prof. P. E. Vernon, Psychological tests in the Navy, Army and A.T.S., *Occupational Psychology*, April 1947, p. 53 (a most valuable paper).

possibilities of further education, and professional advancement. If we are dealing with the operator area, then obviously the first three or four categories (dealing with immediate work content) become important, but as we move to the more able and long-term people, on whom we can afford to spend money for development, then, of course, the upper end of this list becomes important. (We have seen this point made earlier, in the chapter of this book on motivation, when research findings suggested that the less able a person is, the more he is interested in short-term immediate satisfactions and the more able he is, the more he looks to long term satisfactions.*)

This idea of the information test will be returned to later in this chapter in the context of the *pre-interview questionnaire* which, in effect, suggests that a person is not a bona fide candidate for a job unless he is knowledgeable about it.

Information interests, then, are an extremely important source of evidence on interests.

Personal preferences

So far we have considered the assessment of interests from the point of view of the outside observer looking in. That is, we have been looking at possible answers to the question, "What do you mean when you say of an individual: *'He is interested in X'*?".

Suppose now we ask the individual to do some introspection and answer the question, "What do you mean when you say: *'I am interested in X'*".?

Strong's vocational interest blank

An American named E. K. Strong said, "An interest is an *attitude of liking*", and suggested that if you have the same pattern of likes, dislikes, and indifferences as a successful lawyer then you should be a lawyer. If you have the same pattern of likes, dislikes, and indifferences as the successful . . . then you should be a . . . , and so on. Having established this, Strong then

* See also L. T. Wilkins, *Occupational Psychology*, October 1949, p. 235.

drew up a large inventory of questions where you were asked to ring one of L (like), I (indifferent), D (dislike) for over 400 questions and your pattern of responses was matched against those profiles obtained for successful people in different occupations. The book, *The Vocational Interests of Men and Women* discusses this approach thoroughly.

The question I would like to raise at this stage is this: Is Strong right when he says an interest is an attitude of liking? If I find myself in a room where an individual is playing about carelessly with a loaded revolver, I am interested in what is going on, but it does not follow that I like it. This means there is also an *attitude of attention* to be taken into consideration.

When we are speaking of interests in another we notice an *attitude of attention*.

When we are making introspections we think in terms of an *attitude of liking*.

The plan we propose combines three lines of evidence:

(a) Observed persistence in behaviour.
(b) Information interests.
(c) Expressions of personal preferences.

The least valid source of evidence is personal preferences—what a person says he likes and dislikes. You may be alarmed at this, but the truth is that the person is saying that he likes the idea of doing what he *thinks* the job is and we cannot attach much weight to this statement until we know that this expression of liking is based on *reality*.

Some years ago a small team* looked into the wastage of student nurses which was over 50 per cent. One of the arguments was that they were disillusioned when faced with reality. A recent advertisement for nursing (for example) showed a picture of a girl standing by the side of a sports car talking to a man in the car. By the side of that advertisement should appear a caption to the effect that: "Nursing is a 365 day a year job, 24 hours a day! How

* Information test for use in the selection of student nurses, *Hospital*, February 1954.

do you think that will affect you?" No person should enter a service industry until they have thought of the effect which this state of affairs can have on their social life.

It is important for people to weigh the satisfactions and frustrations likely to be achieved in a job before their expressions of liking can be taken as ensuring adequate motivation. This means that we must match *expressions of liking* against *information possessed* about the job. If these two agree, then we can turn to reports from referees for any evidence likely to confirm the choice, from the aspect of observed persistence in behaviour.

If *expressions of liking* are confirmed by *information* and *reported interests*, then we can be assured that the individual is adequately motivated; the problem then is to say, "Is the person physically and intellectually suited for the work and can he comply with the special circumstances clause?"

Order of precedence

As far as order of precedence in selection is concerned we could well start by considering the special circumstances clause. If this cannot be met, we need not proceed. The next point to consider is interest—adequate motivation and then the intellectual and physical qualities which will set the ceiling of performance in the field of adequate motivation.

(It can be seen now what a difficult task the chairman had taken on when he said he would look at work interests; but at the same time it shows what "good observers" "good chairmen" sometimes are, because they often do something very much as in the procedure recommended.)

Pre-interview questionnaire

Consideration of the information interest area has led to the design of pre-interview questionnaires. In my experience these have included key questions on motivation areas in particular—significant areas of possible satisfaction and frustration. These pre-interview questionnaires are completed by the candidate prior to the interview and are scored whilst the candidate is being taken on a tour of the establishment and work situation (often intended as a 1 : 1 interview on the job). The questions which show evidence of lack of information, or wrong information, are ringed and used for discussion in the interview. For example, in a supervisor questionnaire: "How do you expect your pay to compare with that of the people you supervise? (a) in a normal week? (b) When overtime is worked in the department?"

If he answers *more* to both (a) and (b), then in some firms he would be wrongly informed, because (b) can be *less*.

The candidate is not rejected on the grounds of faulty answers, but is "put right", so to speak, about the actual conditions obtaining in the field. If he now decides to withdraw, then we have lost a person who would have been frustrated in any case. On the other hand, if he rationalizes the situation and looks for compensation in alternative sources of satisfaction, then we are sure that we have a bona fide candidate. The questionnaire shows the candidate (and the panel members) what he does not know about the job; information which he should possess before he commits himself.

This kind of questionnaire can in itself be used as a *pro forma* for an interview because all the questions on it need to be answered at some time.

We have also employed this kind of questionnaire to trigger off student activities in induction courses into technical education and in connection with careers work. The questionnaires ask vital questions to which answers must be found from the study of career literature and other information sources.

Leadership

We, of course, no longer believe that leaders are born in selected families and trained in certain kinds of establishments. Two world wars have established that leaders arise in situations because of the particular qualities they possess which are relevant to the situation. If I break my leg it will be the person in the group who knows something about first aid who will lead the group by virtue of his special knowledge. I have had an experience where a girl working for me injured herself badly, but she led the group by telling them what to do with herself because of her own knowledge of first aid.

If we accept this view, then, of course, the problem of leadership selection amounts to finding which of a number of candidates will lead in a situation which is very much like the work situation. This is the origin of some parts of group selection procedures, where, in effect, all the candidates are observed by a panel when working on a common problem, particular leadership character-istics being rated at the time.

Some time ago we had an exercise on the merging of three development departments. An official concerned with the event came along with plans and details and set the problem to the groups. He then arranged for consultants to come along to be questioned for further information. He then said to the groups: "Your job is to plan this merger dealing with all the technical, organizational, political (tactical), and social problems and report back to us on Friday afternoon what you have decided."

Now if observers had sat in with or worked alongside these groups, then they would have been in a position to rate the kind of intelligent decisions they knew were at a premium in the job. (They need not *define* these decision areas; it is sufficient for them to be aware of the fact that this kind of thing is important in doing the job.) This would be a practical intelligence test situation with a five-point rating as a ruler.

In actually doing this kind of work *indirectly*, that is by putting people into role-playing situations of other types, e.g. selection interview, committee procedures, negotiation exercises, I have seen characteristics exhibited by persons which I had never seen before—some of which made me realize that I had completely underestimated the individuals concerned.

This work confirms the view that personality is relevant to an environment and it is reasonable to observe the personality traits relevant to the situation in which we hope to employ people.

The W.O.S.B. and C.I.S.S.B. procedures are relevant here.*

Assessing performance

In assessing the performances of individuals at work, the terms industriousness, enthusiasm, initiative, and the like are still quoted on schedules. I should like to stress that these characteristics are only relevant to the situation in which the judgement was made and the existing level of rating is no criterion of what it would be in *another situation which is different*, i.e.:

> We are not industrious in *all* things.
> We are enthusiastic about *some* things.
> We show initiative in *some* situations.

(We have been able to establish in a research in a school,† for instance, that individuals ranged widely in their application to different work situations and that a *generalized rating for industriousness* did not differentiate between children and therefore would be useless as a personality trait.)

It is important to recognize, however, that such traits as industriousness, enthusiasm, and initiative can be used as *indicators of interest areas* in providing evidence in the category of observed interests, i.e. observed persistence in behaviour.

Because of this variability in attitudes, I prefer to go for interests and assume that the attitudes will be as favourable as possible if the individual is employed in an area where he is interested, i.e. adequately motivated.

Concluding this section I attribute very considerable importance to the assessment of interest and especially to the use of the pre-interview questionnaire. On the intellectual side I would set great

---

* M. A. B. Wilson, The work of the Civil Service Selection Board, *Occupational Psychology*, **22** (4) (October 1948). B. S. Morris, Officer selection in the British Army 1942–1945, *Occupational Psychology*, **23** (4), 219 (October 1949). P. E. Vernon, Validation of Civil Service Selection Board Procedure, *Occupational Psychology*, April 1950, p. 75.

† Henry Gotch Junior School, Kettering. Headmaster: Mr. E. R. Corby, 1955–56.

store by group activities to assess the appropriate types of intelligent behaviour in practical and relevant life situations.

Furthermore, I would like to restate the order of priority in procedure.

> *Firstly*—special circumstances clauses.
> *Next*—assess interest areas.
> *Finally*—intellectual and physical qualities.

We can often accommodate a range of ability, but we ought to aim for adequate motivation first.

In a way some current selection/interview procedures conform to this pattern of priorities when the work is split between the Personnel Department and the Consumer Department. For example:

(a) *Interview with Personnel Department* (1 : 1)
   (i) To cover *special circumstance factors* in the main, i.e. are conditions of service acceptable?
   (ii) *Interest areas*—assume candidate has *volunteered for work he is interested in*. Check this expression of liking against information.
(b) *Interview with Department concerned* (1 : 1)
   To check *intellectual* and *physical* demands and present *attainment* levels.

Finally, in management development—Interest, i.e. adequate motivation, is the key.

The Implication of Personality Traits in the Teaching–Learning Situation

The recommendations of the various training boards following upon the Industrial Training Act 1964 have emphasized the need for instruction in approved training programmes to be conducted by trained instructors and lecturers.

The chapter of this book on habit has looked at some of the problems of practical instruction. The present section reviews theoretical instruction and public speaking, and an appendix is attached to consider the problems of discussion group leading—on the assumption that training has concern for skill, knowledge, and attitude.

Why teaching–learning situation?

If we consider the most economical method of communication orally, as far as time is concerned, then I think you will agree that this is the professional paper. Here the speaker makes his points economically, adheres very closely to his paper, and, in fact, often reads it. He may not look at his audience, except casually, and certainly does not adjust what he says to their reactions. In fact, possibly the only difference between him reading the paper and you reading the text is that he may emphasize certain words or phrases differently and so introduce a particular shade of meaning. The point I want to make is that in the professional paper there is little interaction between the audience and the speaker.

But as we move more into the realms of lecturing, and especially the kind of lecturing one gets in the technical college, the lecturer begins to take note of the reactions of the course members and may begin to modify what he intended to do. He cannot do this too much because he is working to a tight programme of lectures to meet a particular syllabus. (In fact if you do adjust very much in some fields, you will find yourself blamed by both the students and other staff members because you have not completed the programme—irrespective of how well the students understand the bits you have done.) In the technical college and such situations, then, we begin to get more interaction.

If we now consider teaching, here the speed of the teacher has to be matched to the level of understanding of the course members and he often does not proceed until he is fairly sure that understanding has been achieved. Hence his techniques are very carefully adjusted to ensure maximum interaction.

The general point which I wish to make, therefore, is that the more we move from the professional paper to teaching, the more interaction becomes the important characteristic of the situations. This means that the "teacher" tends to learn from the feedback and so the teaching situation is more that of a teaching–learning situation. Accordingly, range, i.e. look at, the group as you work to see what is happening.

Sketching this out diagrammatically we can see a teacher trying to instruct an individual and he himself learning from the individual. We can also see the teacher instructing the rest of the group and learning from the rest of the group. We can also see the teacher teaching through the other members of the group and in effect the group instructing the individual and in turn learning from the individual (Fig. 17).

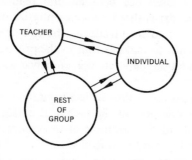

Interactions in the Teacher–Learning Situation

FIG. 17.

Teachers/lecturers in such establishments, where feedback operates, soon face this situation in their contacts with groups. It can be very embarrassing for a young teacher who thinks he has the answer to be told by a student—"But, Sir, we don't do that any longer in our firm." He can learn from current industrial developments and sometimes must learn to harness this new source of information for the benefit of the other course members and to admit that now he, too, is a learner and the student the teacher.

Arrogance is out of place, and if you are dealing with adults, in particular, remember the situations can, and often will be, easily reversed.

Implication of Personality Traits

Now let us consider how the personality traits of the group members will affect our planning of our instruction.

Physical traits

The first thing we need to know about the group members is can we communicate with them? Have they a full complement of the senses, corrected or otherwise (spectacles, hearing aids, etc.), because this will determine the extent to which they can participate.

However, it is important to remember, also, that we can start with a group of individuals with a full complement of senses yet handicap them by bad positioning of material, e.g. demonstrating on the flat; failing to hold things up high enough for people to see; demonstrating to people over a table so that everything is in a mirror image for the observer; visual aids badly positioned; teacher standing in such a way that he isolates part of the group; noisy premises and the like.

Physical traits can also limit skill.

Generally, then, *physical traits limit skill and participation.*

Decide about the working place beforehand.

Interests

Now if I know I can communicate with an individual, the next thing I want to know is Will he pay attention? What is he likely to be interested in?

Sometimes I can guess this, but sometimes I have to make inquiries, i.e. write to the sponsor and ask about a strange group.

Again, if I know what the people are interested in, it is sometimes necessary to show the significance of the proposed activity for this central purpose of the course members. The following example illustrates this.

I once took a new group of automobile engineers for a City and Guilds course in mathematics. They were older people coming back to the technical college in order to further their jobs after a long absence from schooling. The syllabus I had to teach started with vulgar fractions and then over a period of time progressed to more advanced mathematics.

You can imagine the depression which could settle on a group who, coming back hopefully and perhaps a little enthusiastically to the educational setting after a long time find themselves faced with vulgar fractions—the very thing they hated at school and were not very good at.

To meet this problem I spent a good half hour before the session writing up a problem on hydraulic presses and sketching the apparatus in use. The problem was a practical problem as to whether there was enough travel on the ram of the press to achieve a certain clearance with particular components. It amounted in the end to the addition and subtraction of vulgar fractions. I was now able to show that this practical problem could only be solved by manipulating these addition and subtraction processes and that therefore we should revise what we learnt years ago about this.

The result was that in three-quarters of an hour or so we had completed one small sum. I had justified attention but achieved no skill in performances. It was then necessary to say, "Well, this is the kind of process we need to practise and so let us try two or three without the problem." The whole attitude here is to justify why people should attend to and take an interest in what otherwise appears to be tedious material. It is this approach which leads to the label practical mathematics, where the illustration is chosen as near as possible to the field of interest of the individual. In the above case, the example, maybe, was not good enough, and it would obviously have been much better if this could have been chosen from the field of automobile engineering.

I know a man who was so concerned about this interest factor that he spent a great deal of his own time on building constructions in order to find practical problems to illustrate his subject, building mathematics. He was determined that no one should be able to say of his work, "What use is this to me?"

Interest, then, determines direction of maximum response.

Intelligence/aptitude

Having made sure that we can communicate with our group and we have a good idea as to how to engage their attention, the next things we need to know before we can prepare a talk are: How fast can we go? How fast will they learn?

Once again we need to get some information on this subject from the sponsor or other observers. Thus it is quite common in a staff room to hear people say of a new group, "What are they like?", and there is a preparedness to adjust on, "Pretty bright this time—a couple of duds at the back."

Now of course, these words only have relevance in known establishments and against a background of the customary language of the person reporting. But what happens for a strange group?

Evidence on the nature of the level of work customary for the group members may give a guide, but occasionally some test or examination results are known and are used for streaming or setting.

A training centre for the N.C.B. in Durham, for instance, could regularly expect an intake of 160 youths at a time. These lads could be put in a rough order of merit for performances on a relevant intelligence test. On the basis of this test they could be grouped either in layers of ability twenty strong, or in the form of a vertical cross-section of all ability, again twenty to a group. The problem for the training officers and instructors was how do we group them for maximum effect?

If we take a vertical cross-section, then the differential speeds of learning will be high, whereas if we layer, we shall reduce differential speeds of learning, but the persons who are at the bottom of the top group will not appreciate how good they are and the person who is top of the bottom group will not know how bad he is, so that the stimulus of the standards set by other people's level of work will not be available.

In discussing these problems the training officers concerned came to the conclusion that for theoretical instruction they preferred to layer (to reduce differential speeds of learning), but for practical instruction they preferred a vertical cross-section with the more able helping the less able.

Of course, this argument can go on indefinitely and is at the bottom of a great deal of discussion centred round streaming or not streaming in schools, but the problem I wish to point here is that, irrespective of what you do, you will still be faced with some range of ability in a group (and consequent differential speeds of learning).

What can we do?

My recommendation is that you should aim for the average and try a variety of approach to the points being made. Some of the varied points may pick up the below average worker, but the different approach will widen the appreciation of the above average worker who understood your point first time in any case. This broadening of the base of understanding is better than the rapid, slender, attenuated approach of pushing the able person at the expense of the rest.

The practical implication here is that we need some material in reserve for the more able people—not new material, but different illustrations of the same idea.

Intelligence/aptitudes govern speed of learning.

Attainment

But having got attention and having estimated the general speed of learning, we still cannot start our instruction because we do not know the present attainment levels. Our treatment can be too elementary or too advanced, but with unfortunate results and so it is important to inquire from available sources the general attainment levels of the group members. Some establishments have gone as far as forming groups called "sets", where people of comparable attainment levels have been collected in order to set the starting levels correctly.

Attainment then tells us where to start our instruction.

Special circumstances

Finally, in our preparations, having bothered quite a deal about the physical setting of the work, the problem of human

interest, the problem of speed of learning, and existing attainment
levels, we can still be in difficulties because some element in the
environment may not be expected:

A fuse or bulb can "go" on a projector.
I've known a case of d.c. current completely wrecking a
rear-projection demonstration.
Pneumatic drills can arrive at the wrong time.
There is no real support for our visual aids.

In all cases we need to improvise. What was the main point we
wanted to make—can we now do it another way?

The experienced lecturer who was faced with d.c. current when
he wanted a.c. was able to improvise using the blackboard, but a
prominent official giving a slide lecture on his experience as an
explorer was helpless when a fuse went in his projector.

*Always be concerned about the work situation until you have
seen it.*

Special circumstance factors, then, dictate compromise.

Figure 18 summarizes these points economically. There
follow a number of practical conclusions, and, on p. 184,
suggestions for a practical scheme for reviewing the work of the
lecturer/public speaker.

Summary of Practical Implications of Educational Theory

We should ask ourselves the following questions:

(1) What physical handicaps are imposed on the students?
(This applies to eye and hearing defects as well as to those
engaged on remedial or rehabilitation work.)

(2) What attempt have I made to engage the attention of the
students? Have I made any effort to show them that the
*topic of instruction has a significance for them? Have I in
fact tried to interest them in the topic?*

(3) What approximate range of intelligence is possessed by my
group? What arrangements have I made to deal with any

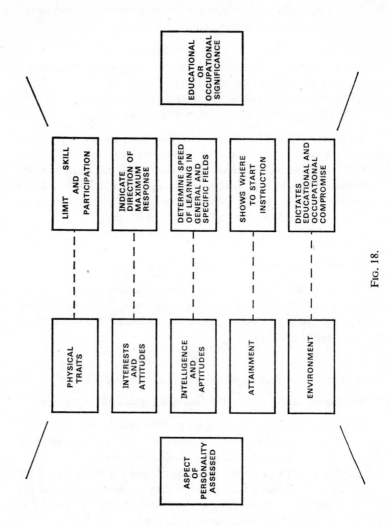

Fig. 18.

unusual large range of intelligence? (*Aim for the average and try a variety of approach.*)

(4) What efforts do I propose to make in order to discover the approximate level of attainment? Where in fact can I start my instruction? (*Known to unknown.*)

(5) Have I allowed for the conditions existing in the place of instruction?

> Is there a blackboard?
> Are there any benches—what apparatus?
> Is it noisy?
> Is it cold?
> Is it depressing?
> Are the chairs uncomfortable?
> Is it cramped?
>
> *Find out about the working place beforehand.*

(6) What training aids are available to support my presentation? Will they appeal to the group or do they just appeal to me?

(7) What attempt have I made to fit my language to the level of the group? Do they know my terms?

(8) What *written or oral exercise* have I to test the ideas communicated by restatement *in the student's own words.*

(9) What degree of stability and span of attention can I expect of the class in view of the general stage of development?

(10) Have I thought of recapitulation and repetition in order to aid the memory?

Refer to these points in your lecture/lesson planning but remember these are only aspects of what is, after all, a *continuous process* of teacher–class interaction.

Effective Speaking in Public

Introduction

There is no ideal public speaker, and the aim of training for public speaking is to make the person conscious of those of his abilities which best enable him to communicate with others and to smooth out those "rough spots" which tend to compete for attention and impede good relationships with the group.

Whilst we do not aim at moulding to a common pattern, we can still evaluate on a systematic plan. It is to our advantage to become aware of such a plan since this can aid us in our study of other speakers and in our own self-evaluation.

Plan of Evaluation

(a) Posture before group.
(b) Speech.
(c) Use of aids including blackboard.
(d) Plan of talk.

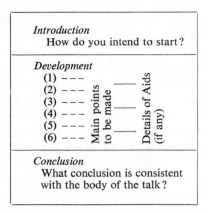

(In the early stages it is a good idea to write out the talk, very fully, beforehand. This will make sure that you can find the right words and illustrations. Now underline in red the main points you wish to make. These should be written on the sheet of paper which represents your notes. Talk from one heading to the next. *Do not read a paper.*)

(e) Speaker/group relationships and interactions.
(f) Speaker's personality.

Most adults possess a considerable body of knowledge which is born of actual experience. It is often our job to organize this body of knowledge to some purpose. An arrogant, dictatorial, authoritarian approach is useless in situations where careful analysis of behaviour and considerable introspection are involved.

The lecture platform is not a place for exhibitionism. I recommend that the speaker concentrates on interesting the members of the group in his subject and not in himself. Can he forget himself in his enthusiasm for his subject? The speaker is a brief visitor; the subject is always there.

Concluding Note

To ME all psychology is social psychology in the sense that no statement about an individual has any meaning without its social/environmental setting. We have no absolute measures of any qualities—only relative judgements and differences.

This book has been concerned with the relationship problems which arise from people working in groups and it was written for people who have some kind of responsibility for persuading people to join in some common activity—sometimes in a formal setting and sometimes informally. It has not been so much concerned with describing groups as with understanding the human relationship problems arising from people working in groups.

The first chapter considered the effective use of human resources in industry and came to the conclusion that work study, ergonomics, and human relations were worthy fields of study in promoting industrial efficiency. The work of Elton Mayo suggested that the human relations aspect of the problem was at least as important as work study and ergonomics in promoting industrial efficiency and, accordingly, represented an essential field of study.

Logically the first problem considered in the human relations field was the introduction of individuals to groups. Habit formation was seen as one of the justifications for the personnel functions of reception, induction, and training—the teaching of those skills which enable the individual to contribute to the work of the group and associate effectively with other people in the group.

The third chapter was concerned with the motivation of people working in groups. Motivation was seen as concerned with a complex of financial (material) and non-financial incentives—

hygiene factors and motivators, hierarchy of needs, if you like—with the important rider that the tokens which are used to recognize performance above the average in a community are culturally based and, of course, can be taught. There is reason to believe that the motivational needs which have their origin in physical survival will become less significant as social legislation advances and movements towards staff status for all labour become reality. The satisfactions which arise from recognition, consultation, and communication will then figure as the prime motivators—the determinants of high morale.

The real difference between staff and labour does not lie in the realm of material rewards but in professional standing—the existence of personal standards of performance; the opportunities for playing some part in determining the working situation and for being better informed about its progress.

The next area considered was that of persuasion and attitude change. The sentiment originating from experiences in other working groups was isolated as the prime factor resisting change. Accordingly, *involvement in decision making* was seen as the solution to the building of favourable sentiments in new working situations. This provides a firm scientific basis for consultation (informal)—one of the "near certainties" in our search for principles governing human behaviour in the context of change.

The word "discipline" has often been associated with sanctions as distinct from mutual recognition of relative responsibilities and goals, but the progression towards staff relationships with all labour, the Donovan Commission* pronouncements on the sanction of dismissal, the growing interest in management by objectives (the *agreeing* of objectives) all point to a more rational approach to discipline—the search for *what* is wrong, rather than *who* is wrong—a concept of appraisal, counselling, and co-operation.

One of the essential criteria for defining a group is the existence of a means of communication between its elements. Accordingly a

* *Royal Commission on Trade Unions and Employers' Associations, 1965–1968*, H.M.S.O., London, ch. ix, § 545, p. 146; § 565, p. 153.

chapter of the book has been devoted to the classes of problems arising in the communication loop as they affect group activity— multiple input channels, division of attention, intelligibility of signals, retention and transfer, chain communication, and feedback. The insecurity which inadequate communication can foster is seen as very real.

The problem of personality and its implications for selection and learning could easily have been chosen as the starting point of this book, but we have been concerned rather with the human relationship problems arising from people already assembled in groups and only later with how they got there. Nevertheless, the outstanding elements in this treatment are, firstly, the dependence of the definition of personality on environment—its changing nature and lack of relevance without environment, and, secondly, the importance of *adequate motivation criteria as the essential element in all selection and management development problems in working groups.*

In conclusion, the case has been made for the importance of installing individuals into the new social setting of the group; for the provision of some say in the kind of activities engaged in; for some recognition of individual performance in terms which are culturally acceptable and the assurance that these individuals be informed of the progress of the common activity.

I believe we shall reach a stage where we shall be ashamed of our misuse of the intellectual powers of our human resources, but in the meantime let us concentrate on adequate motivation in our work situations, for after all our ceilings of performance will only be set by our intellectual and physical qualities in a field of maximum motivation.

APPENDIX I

An Outline of an Approach to Industrial Psychology using the Factors Affecting Productivity as the Central Theme

The Factors Affecting Productivity

Productivity depends directly on the efficiency of the workers and on the industrial conditions under which they have to work.

Industrial conditions can irritate or enthuse the worker and hence affect the personal efficiency. This affects productivity indirectly.

The important triangle in industry is, therefore:

Personal efficiency   Industrial conditions

Productivity

Figure 19* shows a number of factors which are our concern in studying personal efficiency and industrial conditions. These logically fall into four groups:

* This diagram was produced in 1948–9 to suggest a systematic approach to the teaching of the "psychological aspects" of the Urwick Report Recommendations (*Education for Management*, H.M.S.O., London, 1947). It shows the interaction between the industrial/technological conditions and human elements in the organization and how they both contribute directly to the achievement of the objectives of the organization. The whole, of course, rests in an environment of economic, technological and social (including legislative) change. Readers interested in developing ideas about organizations in greater detail are recommended to the book *Organizational Psychology*, E. H. Schein, Prentice-Hall, 1965, especially to chs. 2, 6, and 7, where the works of E. L. Trist, *Organisational Choice*, London, Tavistock, 1963, A. K. Rice, *The Enterprise and its Environment*, Tavistock, 1963, G. C. Homans, *The Human Group*, New York, 1950, R. Likert, *New Patterns of Management*, New York, 1961, E. Katz, *Personal Influence*, Free Press, 1955, and R. L. Kahn, *Organisational Stress*, Wiley, 1964, are briefly collated.

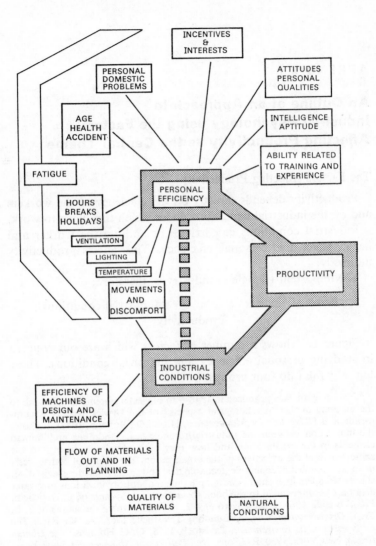

Fig. 19. The factors affecting productivity.

(a) Factors affecting fatigue, boredom, and accident.

(b) Factors affecting selection.

(c) Those industrial conditions which affect the worker:

    (i) Directly—lighting, temperature, hours of work, discomfort and the like.

    (ii) Indirectly—design and maintenance of machinery, planning, materials and natural conditions.

Figure 19 illustrates Elton Mayo's concept of a total situation, and warns against the undue study of any one single factor in isolation.

We see that management (standing at productivity) needs to delegate responsiblity in the interests of productivity and that thereby a number of "services" are created.

It is the duty of supervisors to make use of such "services" created in the interests of productivity (Fig. 20).

The principle of delegation carries with it the obligation to give credit where due.

We see here that such services as welfare, medical, safety training, selection, and the like are at minimum aimed at productivity, just as are those of the engineering and planning departments.

It is likely, however, that work done in aid of some of these "services"—lighting, heating, general discomfort, medical, welfare, and the like—will be interpreted by the worker as evidence of the fact that "he matters" in the organization.

They will thus provide good reason for "identifying self with the purpose of the group", i.e. act as an incentive.

The force of the Western Electric Experiments (Hawthorne Experiment) is shown here.

Generally speaking, the industrial psychologist would stand in Fig. 19 where the words personal efficiency appear, illustrating the viewpoint that industrial psychology is the study of the human being in the industrial environment (Fig. 21).

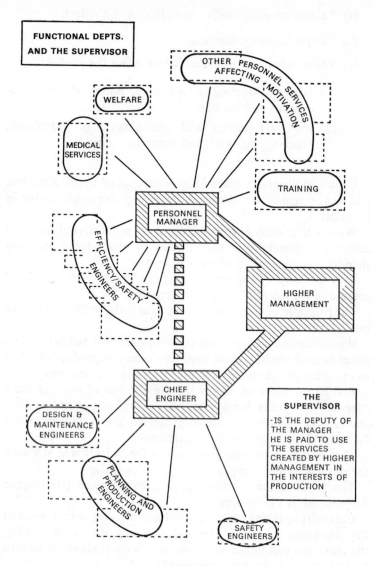

FIG. 20.

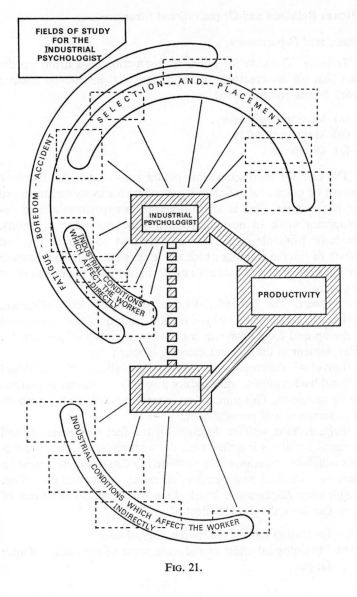

FIELDS OF STUDY
FOR THE
INDUSTRIAL
PSYCHOLOGIST

SELECTION — AND — PLACEMENT

FATIGUE - BOREDOM - ACCIDENT

INDUSTRIAL CONDITIONS
WHICH AFFECT
THE WORKER
DIRECTLY

INDUSTRIAL
PSYCHOLOGIST

PRODUCTIVITY

INDUSTRIAL CONDITIONS WHICH AFFECT THE WORKER
- INDIRECTLY

FIG. 21.

Human Relations and Organizational Structure

Functional Departments

Training. The case for practical instruction rests firmly on the fact that we are creatures of habit. Practical instruction ensures work habits conducive to:

(a) Maximum efficiency.
(b) Maximum safety.
(c) Discipline.

The case for theroretical instruction rests on the fact that one cannot be taught rule-of-thumb procedure for every circumstance we might meet. This is obviously true in experimental and development work. In normal production and operation situations, the basic principles and ideas are the best counter to the bad effects of dilutee training which are largely due to rationalization on the part of the individual and to inadequate communication in general.

Personnel. The fact of individual differences in intelligence, aptitudes, attainments, physical skill and qualities, emotional make-up and local environment, makes selection of personnel a vital element in the efficient use of a labour force.

Individual differences in desires—the effects of individual cultural backgrounds, will produce a variety of individual motivational problems. This impacts on incentive schemes and methods of supervision and management.

Welfare. True welfare depends on the fact that personal and domestic problems interfere with the work situation. Any procedures which can be reasonably instituted to counter these drains on energy are justified on grounds of efficiency, safety and discipline.

Efficiency Engineering. Work done on physical conditions of work can have the double effect of:

(a) Increasing morale, i.e. psychological effect.
(b) Physiological effect of reducing some of the causes of true fatigue.

We should remember that, generally speaking, "morale is more important than the physical conditions of work" (see Elton Mayo), but that with the "human machine" there are still "human tolerance limits" (see Bartlett).

Design and maintenance engineering, planning, safety engineering. These are traditionally the well-accepted functions of industry.

The change in emphasis since the war is that the functions associated with personal efficiency have come into as clear a focus as those associated with traditional technical management. This is a direct consequence of full employment and a major change of motivation from, "You are lucky to have a job", to, "Will you co-operate with us in a joint effort to produce/operate?"

APPENDIX II

A Comprehensive
Selection Procedure Outline*

THIS appendix describes a complete selection procedure used in the mining industry in the early years of nationalization in connection with selection for further education.

The material attached is a reproduction of the paper read by the author to the British Association, Section J, on 31 August 1950, on this topic.

The work described is not severely dated and many of the procedures described could be recommended today.

Selection for Further Education in the Mining Industry

Introduction

It was estimated that between 15,000 and 20,000 youths would be required to enter the mining industry of Great Britain per annum, in order to maintain an adequate labour force. It was agreed, further, that of this 15–18-year-old age-group some 20 per cent would need to undertake further education in the mining and technical schools with a view to providing a recruiting ground for the future underground officials and tradesmen of the industry.

The main problems posed therefore were:

(a) How to select the most suitable 20 per cent.
(b) How to divide this number roughly into two halves:
    (i) potential officials;
    (ii) future tradesmen (electrical and mechanical trades).

* This paper was reproduced in the *Colliery Guardian* in November 1950.

In discussing the pilot work which was undertaken, it is necessary to bear in mind a number of additional facts.

Firstly, the Ministry of Fuel and Power in its Training Regulations demanded that every youth undergo a period of preliminary training (6 months spread over 2 days per week or 16 weeks concentrated). The National Coal Board had established for this purpose some eighty practical training centres in the various parts of the country, each with a training centre manager and a staff of practical instructors. Thus, although the new entrant population was likely to be well distributed throughout the country, all youth entrants would pass through the hands of the training centre managers in the practical centres.

Secondly, when finally posted to a mine, the youth would come under the direct supervision of the training officer at the pit. Approximately 800 such training officers would be involved, but would be in an admirable position to conduct follow-up work.

Thirdly, in most divisions (Durham the main exception) the theoretical instruction in the preliminary training scheme was undertaken by the local education authority in the mining and technical schools. Thus there existed another body of people who were likely to have views on the suitability of the new entrant population for further education.

Fourthly, a central staff college existed at the time, at Nuneaton, at which all the National Coal Board training personnel could receive appropriate training.

Thus it was logical that the selection scheme should be initiated from the central staff college and that the support of the training centre managers, training officers, and local education authorities be enlisted.

Methods

An approximation to a "job analysis" of further education was undertaken, using something like the N.I.P.I. seven-point plan. It will be seen from Fig. 12 (p. 145) that this involved a medical report; that we relied mainly on tests for intellectual qualities (but see later); controlled reports for interest in and attitudes towards further education; a combination of information tests, reported interests and interviews for interest in trades; and interviews and unofficial reports for special circumstances.

The kind of significance these separate items had for us is briefly indicated in Fig. 18 (p. 182).

The important point to note here is that the selection relied on no single method in isolation but on information from tests—reports—interviews—pooled and examined for consistency. Let us consider each group in turn.

Recommendation on Intellectual Grounds

In considering the requirements of the technical school on the intellectual side, it was argued that the individual should possess at least average intelligence for the group concerned and achieve average attainment in English and arithmetic.

Accordingly, a non-verbal intelligence test and four attainment tests were constructed and each individual was rated on a five-point scale, on performance in each of the five tests separately.

> A—top 10 per cent of group
> B—next 20 per cent
> C—next 40 per cent
> D—next 20 per cent
> E—last 10 per cent

The ratings were then entered on a form designed for the purpose, where it was usual to record the names of the youths in order of the scores in the intelligence test (Fig. 22).

An individual scoring A, B, or C in all five tests separately was then awarded a + in the column marked "Recommendation on intellectual grounds". The remaining names were then considered and in the case of any person deemed not to have done justice to himself, on temperamental or other grounds, a ⊕ was awarded on the evidence of three independent reports to that effect.

At this stage it is important to note that:

Name	Colliery	Age	Date of birth	Intell. T.	Mech. Arith.	Arith. Prob.	Series T.	Words T.	Recommendation on intellectual grounds	Recommendation on grounds of attitude (S.M. or U.)	Elec. Eng.	Mech. Eng.	Gen. Eng.	Reported interests	Final recommendation	
Simpson, G.	Lynemouth	15,6	—	A	C	B	C	A	+	M	0	—	—	—	—	—
Parker, M.	Woodhorn	16,7	—	A	A	B	B	B	+	M	0	+2	+2	—	—	—
Ross, A.	Ashington	15,4	—	A	A	A	A	A	+	S	+1	+2	0	—	—	—
Jordan, D.	Linton	17,0	—	A	C	C	B	C	+	U	+1	—	—	—	—	—
etc.																
				B	C	C	B	C	—	U	0	+3	0			
				B	C	C	B	C	—	M	—	—	—			
				B	C	B	C	D	+	U	—	—	—			
				B	D	D	C	C	+	U	—	—	—			
				C	B	B	B	C	—	M	—	—	—			
				C	B	C	B	C	+	S	—	—	—			
				C	C	C	D	D	+	U	—	—	2			
				C	C	B	C	C	—	U	0	0	1			
				D	D	D	C	D	+	U	1	1	—			
				D	E	E	E	E	—	U	—	—	—			

⊕ discuss

FIG. 22.

(a) No great precision in scoring was demanded, in that coarse broad grouping was in use.

(b) No averaging was employed—each individual had to achieve the minimum standard in each of the tests separately. Thus very good English was not allowed to compensate for poor arithmetic.

(c) The rating "C" was the minimum standard.

A variety of early trials had shown that this procedure usually reduced the group to about 40 per cent of the original population on account of the inter-correlations between the various tests.

Thus, we had roughly 40 per cent of the group recommended on intellectual grounds only.

Recommendation on Emotional Grounds

It was now necessary to get some definite idea as to whether the youths would be likely to co-operate in the proposed further education and be interested enough to apply themselves to some effect. It was argued that the collection of ratings of a number of personality traits like "industry", "enthusiasm", "co-operative-ness", etc., was likely to be difficult and the different weights attributed to these items by different persons in the combination of such elements, would render such a scheme unworkable. It was decided, therefore, to let each person combine his own traits in his own proportions and call for controlled reports as under.

Having regard to this person's interest in and attitude towards further education (ignoring intellectual fitness) approve one of the following:

S		Should benefit from further education
M		Might benefit
U		Unlikely to benefit

Three such reports were obtained for each person. Ideally these would be training centre, training officer, local education authority, but it was not always possible administratively to achieve this end, in which case two reports were obtained from different individuals in the practical centre.

The separate S.M.U. reports were then combined into one single S.M.U. recommendation and an entry made on the form (Fig. 22) in the appropriate column.

The number of $\oplus$ cases was now reduced to 20 per cent by deleting the U's and discussing the M's, e.g. it was suggested that a person with M and C level intelligence—both the lowest grades still retained—should be considered for deletion.

Thus by a combination of the two recommendations we were left with 20 per cent of the original population recommended on intellectual and attitude grounds.

The first half of the problem was solved—it now remained for us to split this group on the basis of recommendation for trades.

Recommendation for Trades

The design of the tests for use in this scheme was considerably influenced by the reports of P. E. Vernon in *Occupational Psychology*, 1947, on "Psychological Tests in the Royal Navy, Army, and A.T.S." Thus it was decided to attempt to assess interest in the trades rather than rely on conventional aptitude tests.

Twenty questions for each of 7 interest groups were arranged in mixed order, 60 of these questions alone referred to engineering trades—20 mechanical, 20 electrical, 20 general engineering. The scores on these questions only were recorded on the form and the recommendations were based on a score above a zero level, this representing a performance distinctly above average for the group concerned. This zero level was determined from the formula:

$$\text{Zero} = \text{mean} + 1/6\text{th range}$$

for each interest group separately.

A positive score in any of these groups, E (Elec.), M (Mech.), G (General) was considered to provide one line of evidence of interest in that particular trade. This was regarded as interest deduced from information. We argued, however, that interest in an activity was often more conventionally deduced from an observed persistence of behaviour. We asked, therefore, on our controlled report forms, for evidence of interest in activities—these we recorded under the heading "reported interests". If these two recommendations were in agreement, then our interview could further develop the theme. If the two recommendations were not in agreement, then the interview was left to solve the dilemma.

Interests in trades then was deduced from a combination of evidence. Information test results—reported interests—interview.

We had thus achieved our end: 20 per cent recommended + an indication of trades.

Training of Field Workers and Early Standardization

As was pointed out earlier, the most convenient place to administer the tests was in the practical centres. Accordingly the training centre managers were invited to attend a fortnight's residential course on testing and problems of assessment.

Sixty-two persons attended the six courses in all. The members of each group actually worked the tests, scored the answers, and criticized the whole. On the basis of this criticism some adjustments were made to the draft test material and instructions for administering and marking the same. The revised material was then tried out in two residential centres in County Durham on some 250 youths. Times were adjusted on the speeded tests and further alterations were made as a result.

The test battery and results to date were then examined critically by some members of the research team at the Cambridge Psychological Laboratory under the direction of Professor Sir Frederick Bartlett. Further adjustments were then made. Additional trials were later conducted at Ashington, in Northumberland, and draft material was printed in bulk for larger scale trials in other divisions.

(To date (1950) some divisions have carried and are carrying out trials in all their centres, whilst in other divisions one centre only is acting in a pilot capacity. One division has made no trials.)

As the work proceeded some further instructions on the interpretation of test results was undertaken in short 3-day courses at the Central Staff College or, alternatively, by means of 2-day conferences in the divisions concerned. A very close contact is now maintained between the centres and the Deputy Director for Recruitment and Training (Mr. Swanney) and his assistant (Mr. Maurice) at Hobart House in London. This close contact enables difficulties in procedure, previously dealt with by the staff college to be gradually ironed out.

At the present time it is possible to begin to think of the use of "norms" for the A–E rating. Since we have not yet reached the stage of scientific distribution of manpower, it is likely that one criterion governing selection for further education in the industry will be the capacity of the local technical college or mining school. In this case "area norms" are likely to be more profitable than divisional or national norms. The use of such norms would do much to ease the work of the training centre managers, especially, and as seems likely, when the zero levels for the information test can be quoted. Large environmental differences are not making very significant differences in zero levels.

Follow-up Work

As many divisions are adopting the 16-week concentrated preliminary training scheme, the training officer is really making contact with the trainee after the selection procedure has been completed. It seems, therefore, that his function will be in connection with the follow-up work. For this reason the basic lectures on tests and selection procedures which were included in the 1st and 3rd training officer courses at the staff college will pay good dividends. Most of these 800 officers will have some sound appreciation of the need for adequate assessment of capabilities and follow-up work. The mutual co-operation of the training centre manager and the training officer is essential to the final validation of the present procedures and it is in this co-ordination of effort that area, divisional, and headquarter training personnel can play their part.

Brief Points on Tests and Aptitude Test Trials

The intelligence test was a single picture of the "what's wrong type". Attention was called to three classes of fault—absurdities, impossibilities, and situations likely to lead to accidents. Some fifty faults could be listed. The scene was a busy industrial yard with a pithead gear in the background to "colour" the scene. A practice test was included. Half an hour was allowed. This time limit was adequate. The test was capable of oral treatment for illiterates.

The *arithmetic tests* were:

(a) *Mechanical arithmetic*—20 questions in each of the four rules—practice test in addition and subtraction only.

(b) *Arithmetic problems*—30, including practice test. All could be worked in the head, although space was provided for rough working. Computation aspects were reduced to a minimum.

(c) *Series test*—20 questions gradually increasing in difficulty —useful for grouping purposes.

All these tests were speeded tests.

English. This was a "use of words" test on the lines of the one described in *Occupational Psychology*, April 1947. Thirty simple words were presented, e.g. "bit" and the youth was asked to show four different uses of the word in the sense of four different meanings. Approximately three-quarters of an hour was adequate for this test. One, two, three, or four different answers were scored with different weights:

1 mark for 1 answer to the question.
3 marks for 2 different answers to the question.
6 marks for 3 different answers.
10 marks for 4 different answers.

The *information tests* involved direct and selective response items and contained 7 groups of questions, 20 to each group, all 140 questions arranged in mixed order. (All engineering questions were in the first 100 questions.) The groups were:

Electrical engineering.
Mechanical engineering.
General engineering.
Science applied to living things.
Literary pursuits.
Physical activities.
Art and music.

No time limit (three-quarters of an hour usually adequate).

Aptitude Tests

More latterly in an endeavour to ventilate the relationship between information and aptitude tests, an aptitude test in two parts has been developed. The two parts were intended to attempt a distinction between the engineers with mechanical and electrical bias.

It was argued that if the pure mechanical engineer did exist, then he must be concerned purely with the geometry of motion—the problems of loci—he must be a "geometer".

The electrical engineer would, however, have much in common with the student of heat engines, the steam-raiser, the hydraulics expert and the stresser—in fact the scientist.

The problem then was to design tests suited to distinguishing the "geometer" from the "scientist" and as with Burt to "measure speed of learning" (*British Journal of Educational Psychology*, June 1947, p. 59, footnote) and as with Cox to avoid dexterity and assembly tests. Thus Part I was mainly concerned with loci problems and deductive reasoning and Part II with educing of relations.

Results of trials to date show that performances at both parts of the test and at various parts of the tests themselves are very self-consistent.

In addition the agreement between aptitude test, information tests (pooled engineering questions), and estimates of understanding of engineering principles is quite close.

Generally speaking, it looks as though the aptitude test as a whole picks what is conventionally regarded as a promising engineering student, but does not do this job much better than the pooled information tests (engineering questions). The aptitude test as yet fails to discriminate between electrical and mechanical trades.

Printed copies of these draft tests are now being prepared for more extensive trials. They are likely to be more acceptable than the information test on the grounds of superficial appearances only.

Finally, this pilot work took 3 years to carry out, not because of the tremendous amount of selection carried out, but because of the need for building up an appreciation of the work in the minds of training and other officials. Much of the time was spent on basic lectures of a background nature and considerable patience had to be exercised when it was realized that a test which was ready in draft form in early 1947 was not given a real trial until 12 months later. Not all divisions of the National Coal Board have taken part in this pilot work even to date (1950). It must be remembered that the "selling" of the scheme has loomed easily as large as the "devising" of the scheme.

Our object has always been to guarantee the miner and the official impartial selection for further education for his son. We are not selecting officials, but are providing a system for selecting for further training those persons who eventually through training and experience will merit consideration as officials.

We are following the advice of Professor Sir Frederick Bartlett, trying things out and seeing what happens. We hope to arrive at a sound scheme, but in the meantime we, and others, are learning.

Institute of Education　　　　　　　　　　　　　　　　　E. W. HUGHES
University College
Leicester

Practical Approaches to Discussion Group Leading

THE material in this section describes practical approaches to discussion group leading using visual material to promote discussion and record findings.

The notes are in two parts:

(a) Aids to get people talking.
(b) Techniques in discussion leading.

This kind of material and approach has been used successfully with all kinds of people from school-leavers to very experienced people in professional groups.

The design, and actual conduct, of this kind of discussion group exercise offers considerable scope for the practice of leadership roles and is a valuable aid to training aimed at the personal development of experienced people.

The techniques are also recommended for use in careers work, youth work, and safety training.

The Place of Discussion and Other Group Work in Changing Attitudes

Introductory Note

The work of Chapter 4 suggests that attitudes are complex structures and that a single appeal such as a lecture/talk, or an article, is not likely to be effective in changing attitudes. Such appeals are likely to deal with some of the "roots", but not with the whole reorientation which is necessary. In other words, *logical appeals do not change attitude. What is needed is a multiple approach to what is a complex problem.*

Discussion group work and group projects, i.e. *group activity in which individuals "feel that they matter"*, seems to supply one kind of answer.

Within the discussion group *logical arguments* will be exchanged but these will be weighted by the prestige of the members of the group. The status system of the group and all the *prestige elements of suggestion* will be inextricably merged with the logical appeals.

But more than this the group will arrive at a decision, and not one imposed from outside. In this case the *sentiment* will be right and the group members will be emotionally, as well as intellectually, identified with the solution.

It seems important here to draw attention to the fact that the persons concerned must make these new discoveries and come to these new conclusions *together*. There is no question here of consultation by representation—no delegation—*the working group must be intact in its discussion and project activities, if effective change of attitude is to be achieved.*

It is obvious that on occasion information must be fed into the group via talks, films, expeditions, and the like, before adequate discussion can take place. The group members need some experience to structure. Changes in attitude will be achieved slowly and will require much patience and understanding. The essential feature is a multiple approach to a complex problem with much group activity. It is well to remember Kurt Lewin's statement "the re-education process has to fulfil a task which is essentially equivalent to a change in culture".

The practical problem is first to get people to talk and then to listen. Accordingly in the following sections we will be concerned with practical devices to get people to talk and then will consider how to control and organize this talking, i.e. techniques in discussion group leading.

A. The Use of Aids to get People Talking in Groups

The types of aids which are suggested in the following pages have been developed out of the work of the Bureau of Current Affairs and a number of free lance workers* and have been worked out in practice in the Coal Board Staff College at Nuneaton, young farmers' clubs, and other youth organizations, schools, industrial education schemes, and with professional bodies.

Four main schemes are outlined, but many improvizations are, of course, possible. Very little expensive material is required—a piece of flannel or Dorset crepe (about 4 ft by 3 ft) or soft wall board is an essential feature, but the rest of the apparatus is improvised from paper (e.g. wallpaper) "cut outs" from magazines, lint, gum, poster paint, and a few map and drawing pins. The initial task is to provide a visual aid which is the centre of attention and to devise a system whereby the members of the group actively manipulate some part of the visual aid and later defend and generally engage in discussion in order to reach some agreement on the final layout of the items displayed.

The importance of the visual aid cannot be over-emphasized and it is essential that the group members should be actively concerned with its manipulation in order to arrive at some agreed conclusion.

Notes on the size of discussion groups and the layout are discussed later, but at the moment it is sufficient to remember that the group should sit in some open formation, horseshoe arrangement, open square, or inverted V-formation and that improvised name cards should be available for new groups. (Use folded paper with names printed in coloured chalk/ink (See p. 219 for further notes on discussion techniques and the problem of leading.)

Aids to get them talking

I—*"For and against" technique;* e.g. *Mary's health.*

* For example, Miss Powlett in W.P.H.O.A. training courses.

Materials required

    (a) Wooden blackboard, or sheet of Essex board or card, or soft wall board; size about 4 ft by 3 ft. Dark background desirable. Easel for support.

    (b) Sheet of thin manilla card, or drawing paper, or wallpaper size about 24 in. by 10 in.

    (c) Set of strips of white paper or card about 8 in. by 1 in.

    (d) Black or red ink or poster paint. Felt brushes or printing pens.

    (e) Box of drawing pins or map pins.

    (f) Some coloured chalk (red, blue).

Instructions

    (a) Draw *Mary* (Fig. 23) in rough outline on blackboard, or on card or paper. If the latter, cut out round the outline when complete. A pin-up girl would do.

    (b) Print on the slips of paper a set of activities, which Mary could engage in, and which might affect her health—one activity to one slip of paper. Use bold printing about ⅞ in. high and solid letters (see suggestions).

    (c) Set up the blackboard or wall board with Mary centrally placed.

    (d) Distribute the slips of paper and drawing pins to each of the members of the group, and ask them to pin the slips on one side or another of Mary, as they think that the activity affects Mary's health adversely, or otherwise. If undecided stick the paper at Mary's feet. Pin it on Mary!

    (e) Now discuss the placings and adjust according to the group decisions. (It may be necessary to take a vote sometimes.)

The final layout represents the conclusion to date at the closure of the discussion.

Modifications and alternative procedure

    (a) This work can be done on a flannel graph in which case the printed slips should be backed with lint fastened with gum. (Black Dorset crepe will do instead of flannel, and a variety of materials can be found to be effective.) Peg board and golf tees also offer an alternative technique with positive location.

MARY'S HEALTH

Unfavourable to Mary   Favourable to Mary

Don't know

FIG. 23.

(b) In the discussion described, prepared slips are given to the group members, but if we want them to supply the material for discussion then give out blank slips and pieces of coloured chalk, and ask the group to print boldly on the slips.

Some suggestions

(Include—some obvious, some debatable, some light-hearted, and those intended for serious examination.)

1. Use lipstick.
2. Take tranquillizers.
3. Sun bathe.
4. Wear 4 in. heels.
5. Learn Judo.
6. X-ray for T.B.
7. Have occasional ½ pint.
8. Become nurse for infectious diseases.
9. Eat plenty of bread and potatoes.
10. Bite finger nails.
11. Become hairdresser.
12. Smoke 20 cigarettes a day.
13. Go to pictures on Sunday.
14. Have breakfast in bed.
15. Take slimming pills.
16. Keep late hours.
17. Go on the stage.
18. Start work.
19. Fit false teeth.
20. Get married.

(With acknowledgements to Miss Powlett, a free lance worker in this field.)

II—*Ladder plan*

Discussion aimed at order of merit, or order of importance: e.g. factors important in choosing a job.

Are these things important to Bill in choosing a job?

1. Clean work.
2. Apprenticeship.
3. With friends.
4. Not alone.
5. Big wage.
6. Prospects.
7. Security.
8. Safety.
9. Variety.
10. Particular job.
11. Short hours.
12. Long holidays.
13. No Saturday work.
14. Near to home.
15. Away from home.
16. Good canteen.
17. Sports Club.
18. Music while you work.

1. **Apparatus**

   (a) Flannel graph (about 4 ft by 3 ft).

   (b) Ladder cut from felt or paper size about 30 in. by $4\frac{1}{2}$ in.

   (c) Eighteen strips of paper each bearing one of the above reasons—print about 1 in. high—bold lettering. These strips should be backed with lint using ordinary gum.

   (d) Cartoon representation or cut out photograph of kind of individual under consideration.

2. **Method**

   (a) Set up ladder and cartoon representation of Bill on flannel graph (see Fig. 24 for general layout).

   (b) Distribute printed slips, one to each person, or one between two, if group is large.

   (c) Ask the group members to place their slips on the flannel graph on one side of the ladder, high or low only, according to how important they would consider the item to be to Bill in choosing a job.

   (d) The distribution of the paper slips on the sheet now represents individual expressions of opinion. They have now to be considered one at a time and moved to the opposite side of the ladder to present an agreed group decision.

   (e) This can be achieved in one of two ways:

      (i) Ask the members of the group if they are satisfied with the initial layout and if not what would they move.

      (ii) Select a controversial item like *big wage* and ask the group to decide on that.

3. **Applications**

   (a) Can be used with prepared slips or blank strips to be completed by group members printing their recommendations using coloured chalk.

   (b) Suitable for discussions on:

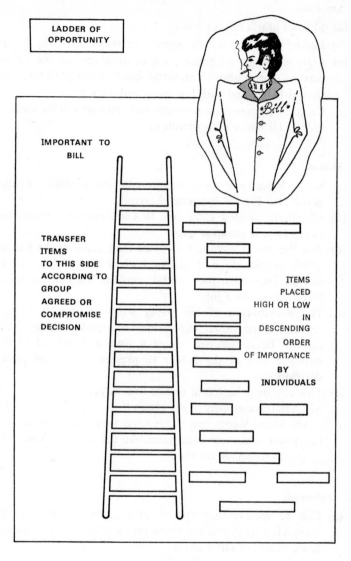

FIG. 24.

(1) Order of items in agenda for a meeting, course programme, or club programme.
(2) Determining orders of priority.
(3) Reasons for joining youth clubs.
(4) Material to be included in recruitment literature.
(5) Discussing possible reasons for leaving firm/club.
(6) Qualities of ideal wife/husband/car/house, etc.

The "ladder" procedure can be combined with the "for and against" technique in ordering material on either side.

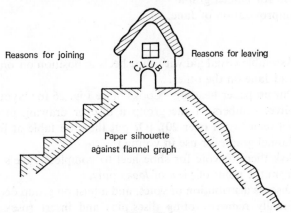

Reasons for joining

Reasons for leaving

Paper silhouette against flannel graph

FIG. 25.

4. Modifications

The ladder can be turned into a set of steps and combined with the other features of the visual aid (Fig. 25).

III—*Classification technique using voting system*
    e.g. *the shoe heel to complete Jane's outfit*

Apparatus

(a) Flannel graph apparatus and about 30 paper discs (1 in. or so) backed with lint; *or*
    sheet of white paper or wallpaper mounted in soft board together with a box of drawing pins.

(b) Improvizations of three shoes showing (i) stiletto heel, (ii) Cuban heel, (iii) low heel. These can be drawn on the paper or cut out and pinned on to the paper or flannel graph.

(c) Five slips of paper with the following headings printed in bold type $1\frac{1}{2}$–2 in. high: (i) looks; (ii) cost; (iii) health; (iv) repair; (v) life. If these are to be used with the flannel graph they could be backed with lint, although they could be pinned if necessary.

(d) Five rosettes improvised by colouring paper—backed with lint for flannel graph.

(e) Improvization of Jane.

Method

(a) Assemble visual aid with shoe heels in position on one side and Jane on the other.

(b) Put up paper heading "Looks" (see Fig. 26 for layout).

(c) Give members of the group a disc or drawing pin (one between two if over 20). [Or put these on table at foot of flannel graph for use in voting.]

(d) Ask them to vote for shoe heel to complete Jane's outfit from the point of view of *looks* only.

(e) Discuss distribution of votes, and adjust on group decision.

(f) Finally remove voting discs/pins and insert rosette (*for looks*) for approved heel.

(g) Put up heading *cost* and repeat. Similarly for health, repair, life, in turn.

Note: Group can vote first and then discuss the array of discs, or can discuss the proposition and then vote.

Applications

Can be used for:

(a) Any discussion determining the relative importances of different items.

(b) Relative merits of car makes/types for stated purposes.

(c) Caveman versus modern man.

(d) Relative merits of the three Armed Services.

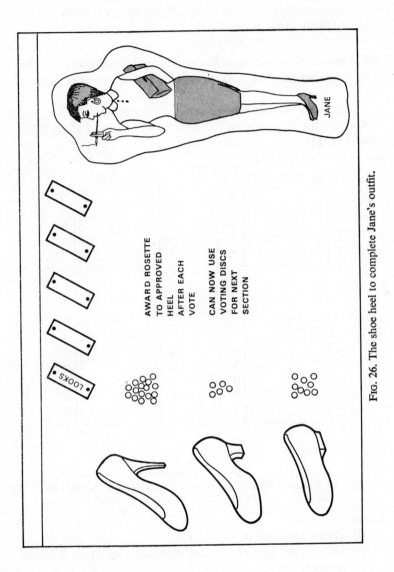

FIG. 26. The shoe heel to complete Jane's outfit.

(e) Subsidiary items of dress in relation to main items.

(f) Milking arrangements.

(g) Type of farm stock/machinery, etc.

This type of discussion is particularly suited to technical problems involving alternative layouts, processes, and equipment.

IV—*Lecture—discussion—reporting back session*

Suitable for large groups (60 or so) and relatively short duration (Fig. 27).

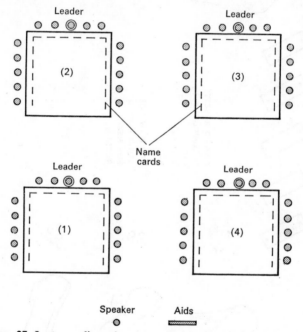

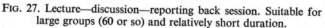

FIG. 27. Lecture—discussion—reporting back session. Suitable for large groups (60 or so) and relatively short duration.

Layout

(i) Tables arranged in four blocks.

(ii) Course members sit around three sides of squares facing speaker.

(iii) Name cards (improvised from folded paper with lettering in coloured chalk—if necessary) particularly for groups unfamiliar with each other.

Procedure

(1) Short talk on vital topic—say "communication" for 20–30 minutes.

(2) Speaker prepares two questions for each of the four discussion groups (questions all different), questions developing some aspect of the theme.

(3) Groups discuss for 20–30 minutes.

(4) Group leaders report back findings or contributions to speaker for comment. In this way all the groups know what was discussed and the general conclusions of the other group members. They are also able to hear the reactions of the speaker—thus developing the theme still further.

Comments

This is an economical way of ensuring the dissemination of a number of ideas, or matters of policy, and of providing an opportunity for some interaction and further follow-up. Linked with consultative and other committees, this represents a method for ensuring that delegates (speaker here) are sufficiently informed of the views of those they represent.

This aids communication of ideas in relation to changes in policy and procedure and employs discussion group techniques to aid assimilation and change of attitude. (With acknowledgements to Mr. Wallace, Training and Education Officer, Messrs. Jones & Shipman.)

B. Discussion Group Leading in General

Introduction

Discussion has been described as organized conversation. This implies the interchange of ideas and information between the various members of the group rather than the passing of information from one particular member to the remainder of the group (as in lecturing). Discussions in technical colleges, especially in relation to technical subjects, has in the past taken the form of question and answer, with the members of the group asking for clarification. Rarely has the teacher been in a position to modify his outlook or emphasis. But now we have coming into the technical college the general subject groups, the management study groups, and the supervisor discussion groups. It is obvious, therefore, that this technique of education—*this meeting of people with varied experience in pursuit of a solution to a common problem*—has to be considered very seriously. And in technical subjects, to offset the tendency to learn rule-of-thumb methods and to rely on the reproduction of set bookwork in stereotyped form (this over-reliance on memory), there is obvious room for discussion, on the basic assumptions, principles, and their general implications in industry and commerce, in the language of the group.

Objects and advantages

(1) The discussion group regards the experience of the members of the group as important and provides a means for the knowledge to be disseminated.

(2) It enables appropriate illustrations in relation to a given topic to be developed to the satisfaction of the individual members. (The leader does not necessarily think of all the good illustrations.)

(3) It forces upon the members of the group the need for clarifying their own ideas with respect to a point and to find adequate means of expressing the same "in their own words".

(4) It gives individual members practice in semi-public speaking, i.e. a chance to make a point before a group of people all listening attentively to what is being said.

(5) It gives the group leader practice in controlling a small group of people and of summarizing what was said.

Both (4) and (5) make discussion groups appropriate to any training course for teachers and instructors in that they provide a gradual introduction to public speaking and group control.

(6) The tendency today towards consultative bodies and committee work in general demands that members be able to conduct themselves reasonably and with tolerance in discussion and be able to sum up adequately at any particular time. Our committee work should not fail because of ignorance of procedure, inability to make a point clearly, or inadequacy of leadership.

Practical aspects

Discussion Group

(1) Groups of 10 to 12 have been found desirable in actual practice—if smaller we lack variety and if much larger there is a tendency for some members to remain silent and to "hide in the group". In a more technical type of discussion (see Conference Method on p. 223) the smaller number is not necessarily such a disadvantage.

(2) Sit so that each can see the others (e.g. circle).

(3) Use printed name cards (e.g. U.N.O. stencil type) in groups where people are not yet familiar with each other—this enables a person to be addressed by name.

(4) A visual aid indicating the main points under discussion is valuable (see section (A) on page 209).

(5) Reference material to hand is an advantage.

(6) The members of the group must respect the authority of the leader.

Group Leader

(1) It is desirable that as many members of the group as possible should have opportunities for leading.

(2) The leader must introduce the topic, break it down into a number of specific sections or questions, and present the problems at the level of experience of the group.

(3) He himself must of necessity join in the discussion especially when it is flagging and a new direction needs to be pointed. However, neither he nor any other member of the group

should hold the floor. For this reason the leader must be aware of his own prejudices and of the particular idiosyncrasies of the other members of the group. He must guard against forcing a special trend in the discussion and must break up any tendency to monologues or duologues by a judicious summing of the views being expressed at the same time and by inviting other members of the group to take up the matter at this level.

(4) The question of when to interrupt and when to permit the exchanges to continue is obviously very significant and depends on experience. This applies equally to the other difficult problems of encouraging the quiet and reticent members to contribute.

(5) It is the duty of the group leader to summarize the main points made by the members of the group. This summary must be as fair and unbiased as possible. The leader is entitled to express an opinion, but only as a member of the group. His authority as group leader refers to the conduct of the group and not to the views of the group.

It is not always possible, or even necessary, to arrive at an agreed conclusion (see conference method for exception).

Types of discussion

(A) Discussion—highly controversial topic (non-technical)

It is obvious that discussion cannot take place unless the members of the group know something about the topic and are not completely agreed. For this reason in early work with discussion groups it is desirable to choose topics of general interest and about which there is likely to quite a diversity of views: e.g.

Should football pools be nationalized?
Should married women go out to work?
Should professionalism be encouraged in sport?
Controversial topics related to course at technical college.

In this way we are assured of plenty of interaction and few awkward gaps demanding the intervention of the leader. It is likely that in this type of discussion an agreed conclusion will not be found, and in this case it is the duty of the lecturer to sum the main points of agreement and of dissention. It should be remembered that these topics may be used in certain training groups for exercise only, in order to familiarize with discussion group procedure.

(B) Discussion—technical problems—conference method

In committee meetings, board meetings and the like, it is often *necessary to arrive at a compromise solution.*

For this reason it is convenient to use a blackboard and proceed somewhat formally as under (Fig. 28).

(1) Aspect of topic	(2) Views of group summed	Agreed compromise conclusion
(A)		
(B)		
(C)		
etc.		

FIG. 28.

It is obvious that some detailed discussion will be necessary to complete columns (1) and (2) and that considerable skill will be demanded of the leader in order to get the members to arrive at an agreed conclusion. It can be seen that this treatment (known as conference method to some people) demands experience of ordinary discussion groups for adequate returns.

This section is most significant in relation to committee procedure.

(C) Short courses—conferences

Management studies and the like

As we stated earlier it is obvious that we should not attempt to discuss something we know little about, or upon which we have little organized knowledge. For this reason quite a number of conferences arrange for a lecture to be given (or paper to be read) on a particular topic and then ask the members to break up into a number of smaller groups—syndicates, etc., in order to discuss the material of the paper or certain specific questions raised by the lecturer. It is common then for each group to decide on one or two agreed questions, or on an agreed statement of a viewpoint, in order that this can be presented to the lecturer for his comments later.

The whole is thus a sandwich:

Paper or lecture—Basic material disseminated by lecturer.
Discussion groups—Questions or contribution decided.
Reporting back—Questions posed to lecturer or contribution made for comment by lecturer.

This procedure is used in many conferences of professional bodies in this country and has obvious advantages in that it enables the members to digest the material of the paper and in the reporting stage to make full use of the presence of an expert. It is obviously likely to fail if the discussion group leading is poor and hence the importance of some training, some briefing, however slight.

Finally

In training for discussion it is valuable to have a short time set aside for review of the discussion and its conduct.

A number of questions should be answered:

(a) in relation to the appropriateness of the topic and technique used;

(b) in relation to the group leader;

(c) in relation to the participation by the group.

(1) *Aspect of topic under discussion* i.e. *headings*	(2) *Important points* emerging with respect to this aspect of the topic, i.e. *details* for consideration by group	(3) *Conclusion* or *compromise*, i.e. agreements or disagreements

FIG. 29. Discussion preparation aid.

Note: In early discussion work the leader may supply cols. (1) and (2) (Fig. 29) and may record several conclusions in col. (3). In later discussion work the leader may get cols. (1) and (2) from the group (using discussion, but tightly controlled). He may have to insist on only *one* compromise solution.

Selected Reading

ALLPORT, G. W., *Personality: A Psychological Interpretation*, New York, Constable, 1937.

ARGYRIS, C., *Personality and Organization*, Harper, 1957.

BARTLETT, F. C., *The Mind at Work and Play*, Allen & Unwin, 1951.

BROWN, J. A. C., *The Social Psychology of Industry*, Pelican, 1954.

BROWN, W., *Exploration in Management*, Pelican, 1965.

COOPER, B. M., *Writing Technical Reports*, Pelican, 1964.

DRUCKER, P., *The Practice of Management*, New York, Harper, 1954.

FLEMING, C. M., *Adolescence*, Routledge & Kegan Paul, 1948.

FRAZER, MUNRO, *Psychology: General, Industrial and Social*, London, Pitman, 1963.

HEIM, A., *The Appraisal of Intelligence*, London, Methuen, 1954.

HERZBERG, F., MAUSNER, B., and SNYDERMAN, B., *The Motivation to Work*, New York, Wiley, 1959.

LIKERT, A., *New Patterns of Management*, New York, McGraw-Hill, 1961.

LUPTON, T., *Management and the Social Sciences*, London, Hutchinson, 1966.

McDOUGALL, W., *An Introduction to Social Psychology*, London, Methuen, 1946 (28th edition).

McGREGOR, D., *The Human Side of Enterprise*, New York, McGraw-Hill, 1960.

MASLOW, A. H., *Motivation and Personality*, New York, Harper, 1954.

MAYO, E., *The Social Problems of an Industrial Civilization*, Harvard University Press, 1945.

REVANS, R. W., *Science and the Manager*, McDonald, London, 1965.

SAYLES, L., *Managerial Behaviour*, McGraw-Hill, 1964.

SCHEIN, E. H., *Organizational Psychology*, Prentice-Hall, 1965.

THOMPSON, G., *Instinct, Intelligence and Character*, Allen & Unwin, 1938.

TREDGOLD, R. F., *Human Relations in Modern Industry*, London, Duckworth, 1949.

TRENAMAN, J. *Out of Step*, Methuen.

UNIVERSITY COLLEGE LONDON, *Communication Research Centre, Studies in Communication*, Secker & Warburg, 1955.

VALENTINE, C. W., *Psychology and its bearing on Education*, Methuen, 1955.

VERNON AND PARRY, *Personnel Selection in the British Forces*, University of London Press, 1949.

WALL, W. D., *Adolescent Child*, Methuen, 1948.

Index